KEYS TO PARENTING A CHILD WITH ATTENTION DEFICIT DISORDERS

Second Edition

Barry E. McNamara, Ed.D.,

and

Francine J. McNamara, M.S.W.,

C.S.W.

BARRON'S

Cover photo by the STOCK MARKET

DEDICATION

In loving memory of Barbara Abrams. She touched many lives
with love.

All inquiries should be addressed to:
Barron's Educational Series, Inc.
250 Wireless Boulevard
Hauppauge, NY 11788
www://barronseduc.com

Library of Congress Catalog Card No. 00-034286

International Standard Book No. 0-7641-1291-0

Library of Congress Cataloging–in–Publication Data
McNamara, Barry E., 1949-
    Keys to parenting a child with attention deficit disorders /
Barry E. McNamara and Francine J. McNamara.—2nd ed.
        p. cm.
    Includes bibliographical references and index.
    ISBN 0-7641-1291-0 (paper)
    1. Attention-deficit hyperactivity disorder—Popular works.
I. McNamara, Francine.   II. Title.

RJ506.H9M425   2000
618.92'8589–dc21

                                                    00-034286

PRINTED IN THE UNITED STATES OF AMERICA
9 8 7 6 5 4 3 2

CONTENTS

~~~~~~

PREFACE

L ong before the label *Attention Deficit Disorder* (ADD) is used to describe a child's behavior, parents know something "isn't right." It may be that he's constantly in motion, or that he cannot concentrate for more than a few minutes, or that he acts first and thinks later. Parents of these children struggle to understand this complex disorder. They know that it affects just about everything the child does. It makes it difficult to make and keep friends, join clubs, participate in sports, function in school. And it has an impact on all members of the family.

Parents turning for help may be overwhelmed with the vast amount of information, some of it conflicting, about this disorder. In this second edition, we have attempted to synthesize the most recent research in the field in order to provide parents with practical solutions to the problems they encounter.

The book is divided into six parts. Part One discusses general issues related to the nature of ADD. Part Two discusses the various components of the diagnostic procedures used to identify ADD. In the third part a comprehensive intervention plan is provided. Part Four provides parents with information and strategies that will enable them to work effectively with schools, Part Five deals with activities outside of school, and Part Six includes a discussion of frequently voiced concerns about ADD.

It is our hope that we have brought some order to the

chaos surrounding the term *ADD*. Parents of children with ADD are presented with numerous challenges. We hope this book provides answers to their questions and solutions to their problems.

We want to acknowledge the many parents of children with Attention Deficit Disorders who have shared their experiences and concerns with us. Their feedback has been gratifying, and we have learned a great deal from them. This book has benefited also from the tireless efforts of our editor, Linda Turner. This is the fourth book that she has edited for us. We thank her. As in everything we do, our wonderful daughters, Melissa and Tracy, continue to be our source of love, joy, and pride.

Part One

~~~~~~

WHAT IS ADD?

Attention Deficit Disorder is very complex. These introductory Keys will provide you with an overview of ADD, the terminology used, the characteristics of the population, how to identify a child with ADD, and the causes of the disorder.

1

OVERVIEW

Attention Deficit Disorder (ADD) is not new. It has been widely discussed in medical, psychological, and educational journals for many years. What is new is the increased interest in the disorder. It seems that everywhere you turn someone is talking about ADD. Local newspapers feature articles on the disorder, national magazines have covered the topic at length, and local and national newscasts have run stories on children who are diagnosed as having ADD. Go into any school and teachers will tell you about their students with ADD; parents will tell you about the meetings they had with teachers where it was suggested that their child had ADD. From the viewpoint of a casual observer it would seem that the matter is fairly simple—a simple diagnosis and even simpler solutions. However, parents of children with ADD or those who suspect their child has ADD know it's much more complex.

There is no definition or treatment upon which all professionals and parents agree. Parents find that they are confused about the meaning of the label "Attention Deficit Disorder." And it's not surprising when you look at the history of ADD. The term ADD refers to a family of disorders. You may have heard or read about other terms, such as Attention Deficit Disorder with Hyperactivity (ADDH), Attention Deficit Disorder without Hyperactivity (ADD/no H), Attention Deficit/Hyperactivity Disorder (AD/HD), or Undifferentiated Attention Deficit Disorder (U-ADD). They all refer to different types of attention deficits.

There is little doubt that the terminology describing children with ADD will change in the future. The terminology has undergone change and revision since the early forties. The characteristics of the children being described, however, have remained fairly constant. Currently, the terms Attention Deficit/Hyperactivity Disorder (AD/HD) and Attention Deficit Disorder (ADD) are both used by professionals in the field.

Throughout this book the term Attention Deficit Disorder (ADD) will be used because it is the most general and describes many kinds of attention deficits. You will notice that not all of the terms listed above include the word "hyperactivity." Unfortunately for many, hyperactivity has become synonymous with ADD. Not all children with attention deficits are hyperactive. There are children who have a hard time paying attention, who cannot stay with one task for a long time and who have a hard time figuring out what is important and what's not. These children will not necessarily be in constant motion, in fact they may be sluggish and withdrawn. They are not hyperactive, but they are inattentive. This group of children probably doesn't receive the kind of interest and concern that children who are constantly on the go do, but they clearly have attention deficits.

In order to best help their child, parents need to understand how this disorder is diagnosed, reasonable approaches that can be employed at home, and how to interact with school personnel. Parents also need to be aware of current issues related to ADD. Parents who are well informed will be able to make sensible decisions about the best approaches to dealing with ADD. Moreover, they will be able to function as their child's advocate in the school.

2

TERMINOLOGY AND CHARACTERISTICS

The terminology has changed over the years and has varied across disciplines. In the 1960s a child with an attention problem evaluated by a physician would most likely be labeled as having *minimal brain dysfunction* (MBD), whereas the school might use the term *learning disabled* (LD) or *hyperactive* (see Key 36 for a discussion of learning disabilities). Currently, the term most frequently employed is *Attention Deficit/Hyperactivity Disorder* (AD/HD). Some experts suggest using the more general term *Attention Deficit Disorders* (ADD) because it includes any kind of attentional problem, not just those where there is hyperactivity.

The most frequently cited characteristics of children with ADD are *hyperactivity*, *distractibility*, and *impulsivity*. They have difficulty staying on task, and focusing on important aspects of conversations and/or school-related tasks. Frequently they do not complete tasks because they are moving rapidly from one activity to another or are distracted by extraneous stimuli. Parents talk of children who require little sleep, are very restless, and are constantly in motion.

Hyperactivity is a specific central nervous system disorder that makes it difficult for children to control their motor activity. These children are not necessarily constantly on the go, but they appear to be restless and fidgety. Parents will tell you about their child who can't sit through a meal or who moves from one activity to another very rapidly or who "never shuts up." Teachers tell you that these students are always doing something. They may be getting up to sharpen their pencil, tapping their pencil or fingers on the desk, tapping their foot on the floor, finishing assignments very fast and often incorrectly, running around on the playground, and squirming in their desks. These behaviors are often without purpose or focus. Frequently, you'll hear someone say "I don't know where he gets his energy" or "I wish I had his energy." This is not the type of energy that allows someone to get a great deal accomplished. Quite the opposite, it interferes with productivity. This term, *hyperactive*, is clearly overused. There are many children and adolescents who move around more than we would like them to but who should not be referred to as hyperactive. It is a term that should not be used casually, but be reserved for those children and adolescents with a specific disorder. Without a multidisciplinary evaluation, it is difficult to judge a child's movements as hyperactive.

Children who are distractible have difficulty staying on task. These children have difficulty filtering information that comes in from the senses. Most of us are able to block out certain bits of information from the environment and focus on what is most important. Unfortunately, children who are distractible are not good at discriminating between relevant and irrelevant information, thus everything competes for their attention. They are unable to focus on a specific task for a long period of time, hence the term *short attention span* is often used to describe them.

You've seen children and adolescents who are easily distracted. A slight noise in another part of the room will draw their attention. They hear someone talking outside the house or above and are distracted by it. A car goes by the window and they rush to look out. They may walk into the bedroom to get something, their attention shifts to a picture on the wall and they will forget what they went to the bedroom for. Many of these children experience difficulty in places where a great deal is going on, such as birthday parties, shopping malls, carnivals, circuses, and the like. Many times they will become irritable and restless because of the increased stimulation in their surroundings. Some classrooms can cause the same problem. There just might be so much going on that the child can't attend effectively.

There are children with ADD who are impulsive. They act first and think later. They may say things that are offensive, but not realize it until it is pointed out to them. We know of a youngster who frequently hits his classmates and then apologizes profusely. He lacks the ability to anticipate the meaning of his behavior and he merely acts out. Impulsive children ask questions that have nothing to do with the current subject of conversation. In class, these children will call out answers before the questions have been asked and usually with the wrong answers. These children and adolescents appear to be accident prone because they do not attend to the consequences of their actions. We know of children who have jumped out of windows, fallen out of trees, and run through glass doors. Many have an incredible number of cuts, scratches, and bruises. The child who truly has ADD will manifest these behaviors in both school and home. One of the hallmarks of the disorder is the pervasiveness of the behaviors displayed. If a child only displays these characteristics in one setting—school or home—then it can probably be attributed to causes other than ADD.

3

CRITERIA FOR IDENTIFYING AD/HD

The criteria for identifying Attention Deficit/Hyperactivity Disorder as stated in the Diagnostic and Statistical Manual of Mental Disorders (DSM IV) of 1994* is listed below:

Diagnostic and Statistical Manual of Mental Disorders, Fourth Edition Attention-Deficit/Hyperactivity Disorder

A. Either (1) or (2):
   (1) six (or more) of the following symptoms of **inattention** have persisted for at least 6 months to a degree that is maladaptive and inconsistent with developmental level:

   Inattention
   (a) often fails to give close attention to details or makes careless mistakes in schoolwork, work, or other activities
   (b) often has difficulty sustaining attention in tasks or

*From American Psychiatric Association: *Diagnostic and Statistical Manual of Mental Disorders*, Fourth Edition. Washington, DC, American Psychiatric Association, 1994.

play activities

(c) often does not seem to listen when spoken to directly

(d) often does not follow through on instructions and fails to finish schoolwork, chores, or duties in the workplace (not due to oppositional behavior or failure to understand instructions)

(e) often has difficulty organizing tasks and activities

(f) often avoids, dislikes, or is reluctant to engage in tasks that require sustained mental effort (such as schoolwork or homework)

(g) often loses things necessary for tasks or activities (e.g., toys, school assignments, pencils, books, or tools)

(h) is often easily distracted by extraneous stimuli

(i) is often forgetful in daily activities

(2) six (or more) of the following symptoms of **hyperactivity-impulsivity** have persisted for at least 6 months to a degree that is maladaptive and inconsistent with developmental level:

Hyperactivity

(a) often fidgets with hands or feet or squirms in seat

(b) often leaves seat in classroom or in other situations in which remaining seated is expected

(c) often runs about or climbs excessively in situations in which it is inappropriate (in adolescents or adults, may be limited to subjective feelings of restlessness)

(d) often has difficulty playing or engaging in leisure activities quietly

(e) is often "on the go" or often acts as if "driven by a motor"

(f) often talks excessively

Impulsivity

(g) often blurts out answers before questions have been completed

(h) often has difficulty awaiting turn

(i) often interrupts or intrudes on others (e.g., butts into conversations or games)

B. Some hyperactive-impulsive or inattentive symptoms that caused impairment were present before age 7 years.

C. Some impairment from the symptoms is present in two or more settings (e.g., at school [or work] and at home).

D. There must be clear evidence of clinically significant impairment in social, academic, or occupational functioning.

E. The symptoms do not occur exclusively during the course of a Pervasive Developmental Disorder, Schizophrenia, or other Psychotic Disorder and are not better accounted for by another mental disorder (e.g., Mood Disorder, Anxiety Disorder, Dissociative Disorder, or a Personality Disorder).

Code based on type:

314.01 Attention-Deficit/Hyperactivity Disorder, Combined Type: if both Criteria A1 and A2 are met for the past 6 months.

314.00 Attention-Deficit/Hyperactivity Disorder, Predominantly Inattentive Type: if Criterion A1 is met but Criterion A2 is not met for the past 6 months.

314.01 Attention-Deficit/Hyperactivity Disorder, Predominantly Hyperactive-Impulsive Type: if Criterion A2 is met but Criterion A1 is not met for the past 6 months.

The criteria lists three types:

AD/HD's combined type, AD/HD Predominantly Inattentive type, and AD/HD Predominantly Hyperactive-Impulsive type.

Most children are diagnosed with the combined type and the predominantly hyperactive type. Note the qualifiers that these symptoms must be present before the age of seven, and they must be present in at least two settings. They must impact on social, academic, or occupational functioning and must not be the result of other disorders.

AD/HD, Predominantly Inattentive Type

Many experts believe this is an overlooked population, and children who are described as "out of it," "spacey," and the like may be ADD. Moreover, some have suggested that more girls than boys are this type and not properly diagnosed. (See Key 39, Girls with ADD)

When you examine the criteria, you can readily see why many professionals and parents have a difficult time deciding on a particular point. For example, "fidgets with hands or feet or squirms in seat." How much? How many times? During what tasks? What do you mean by squirms? And on and on. Russell A. Barkley, Ph.D., cites a number of concerns regarding the DSM IV criteria in his excellent book *Attention Deficit Hyperactivity Disorder: A Handbook for Diagnosis and Treatment*. However, he notes that is a vast improvement over previous criteria and is closer to the specific literature on ADHD. He advises professionals to not be dogmatic when adapting the criteria and to use good clinical judgment.

Identifying a child with ADD is often a process of exclusion. That is, when other difficulties have been ruled out and the child exhibits characteristics such as distractibility, hyperactivity, and difficulty staying on task, the diagnosis is commonly ADD. However, this diagnosis should never be made in isolation or by one person. A proper assessment uses the team approach, whereby professionals from medicine, psychology, education, and social work evaluate the child/adolescent together. This multidisciplinary approach will be discussed further in this book.

4

CAUSES OF ADD

For good reason, parents often want to know why their child has an ADD. What makes him move around constantly? Why can't he sit still? He can't seem to pay attention, why? These and many other concerns expressed by parents often have professionals feeling somewhat frustrated because there is no single cause for the constellation of behaviors attributed to ADD. However, there is a consensus among professionals in the field that ADD is most likely caused by the interaction of biological and psychosocial factors. Larry Silver, M.D., notes that although the child's genetic makeup or other prenatal, perinatal, or postnatal factors provide the biological basis for this disorder, the manifestation of behaviors associated with ADD is also influenced by culture and environment. There is also a strong hereditary component to AD/HD.

Because the term *ADD* has become "popular," parents have to be careful about misdiagnosis. That is, the diagnosis of ADD cannot be made by one person, and both biological and psychological factors should be present. The only way to decide whether or not your child has ADD is to have him evaluated by a group of professionals who look at all aspects of your child's development and behavior. This team, referred to as a multidisciplinary team, consists of a medical doctor (neurologist), a psychologist, a special educator, and a social worker. This team works together to find out what is causing your child to have difficulty. There are many reasons why a child is inattentive, most of which are not due to an ADD. There are children who are hyperactive, impulsive and/or distractible because they are under a great deal of stress. Because of this stress a child may be irritable and impulsive, she may daydream and appear to be in "another world." Clearly, this problem must be addressed, but it is not an ADD. Other children may have characteristics of ADD because they are depressed. They may be agitated, restless, withdrawn, in "their own world." They may have a hard time paying attention and concentrating. Once again, this is a serious problem that must be addressed, but it is not ADD.

Throughout this book when we refer to ADD we are referring to that group of children and adolescents who have been diagnosed based on the results of a multidisciplinary evaluation and whose behavior is caused by the interaction of biological and psychological factors.

Part Two

‹‹‹

DIAGNOSIS OF ADD

A thorough multidisciplinary evaluation is crucial for the accurate diagnosis of ADD. Medical, psychological, educational, and social history evaluations must be undertaken. Each component of the evaluation, as well as ways to evaluate all the findings, will be discussed in the following Keys. Disorders occurring simultaneously, known as comorbidities, will also be discussed.

5

THE MULTIDISCIPLINARY APPROACH

A DD is a complex disorder. In order to insure a proper diagnosis, information must be gathered from a variety of sources. The evaluation should be undertaken by a group of professionals, referred to as a multidisciplinary team. This team consists of a physician (neurologist), a psychologist, a special educator, and a social worker. They work together in making a diagnosis that will provide you with a total picture. Without a multidisciplinary approach, an important part may be missing. And without that part, an erroneous diagnosis may be made.

The *neurologist*, preferably a developmental or pediatric neurologist, will evaluate the functioning of the central nervous system. This is not an invasive examination. Depending upon the nature of the concern, certain laboratory tests may be desirable. For example, if there is a suggestion that there is a seizure disorder, the neurologist may ask for an electroencephalogram (EEG), which measures brain wave activity. This is also a painless, noninvasive test.

A *psychologist* will evaluate the intellectual and social-emotional functioning of the child. The psychologist will look for disorders such as learning disabilities, emotional disturbances, or other psychological or psychiatric disorders that may exist with ADD or may be the main problem.

A *special educator*, thoroughly trained in psychoeducational assessment procedures, will administer a battery of tests to explore the existence of a learning disability or other school related disorders. The student will be assessed in basic psychological processes (attention, memory, perception) and basic skill subjects (reading, math, and so on) in order to determine specific strengths and weaknesses. In some parts of the country, a school psychologist will administer these tests.

The *social worker* will meet with the family to obtain information about the child's social history including birth information, developmental milestones, family dynamics, medical information, and school placement. The social worker will also explore the behavior of the child at home and at school in order to acquire information that would help determine the cause of ADD.

The need for such a multidisciplinary evaluation cannot be minimized. By accumulating information from a variety of professionals, the true nature and needs of the child can be determined. For example, a child may be referred for an evaluation because of excessive motion in the classroom. Upon evaluation, the neurologist may not find a satisfactory explanation for the behavior, but the special educator may note the school problem as does the psychologist. The social worker would request a home visit and the mother may confide in her that there are marital difficulties and she has been under a great deal of stress. In such a case there does not appear to be a neurological basis to ADD. Rather, the child's anxiety about her parents is causing her to act in a disruptive manner in the classroom. The treatment would be markedly different for this child than for a child who appears to function in a hyperactive fashion because of a central nervous system dysfunction.

When all professionals have accumulated their findings, they generally meet to discuss their results, to determine the existence or absence of ADD, and to develop a treatment plan and ways to monitor progress.

The following Keys in this section will provide more specific information on each component of the multidisciplinary evaluation.

6

THE MEDICAL EVALUATION

The medical examination consists of three major components: (1) the medical interview, (2) the physical examination, and (3) laboratory tests. The medical interview will allow the physician to see if there are other medical conditions that may seem like ADD and/or disorders that occur simultaneously (comorbid). Also, if medication is indicated, it is very important to determine if the child has any medical condition that would interfere with the specific medication.

The multidisciplinary evaluation is best done at a university-based medical facility or a teaching hospital. Many hospitals have established clinics that provide this kind of thorough evaluation. If this is not available to you or if you prefer to work with an individual practitioner, you should ask your physician the following questions:

- What does the evaluation include?
- How much experience do you have with children or adolescents with ADD?
- Will you consult with other professionals before a diagnosis is made?
- If medication is prescribed, how will you monitor the effectiveness?
- Will you consult with teachers to measure the effectiveness of the intervention?

Unless you are satisfied with the answers you are better off finding another physician. You want to make sure that all members of the multidisciplinary evaluation team work for the benefit of you and your child. The medical evaluation is critical in the diagnosis of ADD. Your assertiveness before you begin the process will insure that it will be a thorough evaluation.

After a thorough medical interview a physical exam is undertaken. Basic information such as height, weight, and head size are obtained and compared to groups of children at the same age. Hearing and vision screenings are done. If a hearing disorder is suspected, parents will be referred to an *audiologist*, a professional trained in the evaluation of hearing, and/or a physician who specializes in ear-nose-and-throat disorders, also referred to as an *ENT* or *otolaryngologist*. If visual problems are present parents will be referred to an *optometrist*, a person who measures vision, or an *ophthalmologist*, an M.D. who specializes in the eyes. Blood tests will be performed and any problems will require additional evaluation.

The neurological exam will look at central nervous system functioning. If any problems are found, more extensive testing will be undertaken. During this exam the physician will also be evaluating the child's speech and language, thinking skills, and coordination, and other motor functioning (for example, catching a ball, hopping, jumping, skipping). Once again, any problems are followed up with more thorough evaluations.

The final part of the medical evaluation is the laboratory tests. There is no test now available that will diagnose ADD. Laboratory tests such as electroencephalograms (EEG), magnetic resonance imaging (MRI), computerized axial tomograms (CT Scan), blood work, urinalysis, and chromosome studies are not routine parts of the evaluation. These should only be used if there is some indication of a specific, treatable medical disorder, such as a seizure disorder. If these are recommended, be sure to ask the physician why, and if you are not pleased with her answer seek a second opinion.

The medical evaluation is a critical part of the multidisciplinary evaluation. It can rule out the presence of other medical conditions and/or mental health disorders. And it will provide valuable information for other members of the team about the appropriateness of medication.

7

~~~~~~

THE PSYCHOLOGICAL EVALUATION

A psychological evaluation should be undertaken by a doctoral level, licensed psychologist, one who is either a clinical psychologist or a school psychologist. The psychologist will administer an individual intelligence test, most often referred to as an I.Q. An individually administered test is very different from standardized, group administered tests. The group administered tests usually require children to write their responses on an answer sheet. An individually administered test is given to one child, and most questions require verbal responses or that the child do something, but there is little or no writing or reading. There are a number of intelligence tests available to the psychologist, and a good psychologist selects the most appropriate test based upon the needs of the student. For example, if a child has speech and language problems, a test would be selected that does not require the child to talk. If English is not the child's native language another type of test may be selected. Generally, however, the two most popular individually administered intelligence tests are the Stanford-Binet Intelligence Scale and the Wechsler Scales.

The Stanford-Binet Intelligence Scale, for use with ages two through adulthood, provides a mental age that can be converted to an Intelligence Quotient (I.Q.) score. Although it presents items that require verbal and nonverbal performance, it tends to have many more verbal items; thus the

Wechsler Scales tend to be used more often.

- *The Wechsler Pre-School and Primary Scale of Intelligence (WPPSI)*. This is used for children who are four to six and one half years old. This test measures a child's verbal skills, nonverbal reasoning abilities, and perceptual motor skills.
- *The Wechsler Intelligence Scales for Children—III (WISC-III)*. This is used for students ages six through sixteen. You may notice that some psychologists use The Wechsler Intelligence Scales for Children—Revised (WISC-R). However, the most recent test (WISC-III) has parts that are helpful in the diagnosis of ADD. Also, the standardized procedures are more up-to-date. It measures verbal and nonverbal performance skills (five parts for each).
- *The Wechsler Adult Intelligence Scales (WAIS)*. If you are the parent of an adolescent, this test would be used because it applies to people from sixteen years through adulthood. This test also measures verbal and nonverbal performance abilities.

If your child is school age, the WISC III will probably be the test she is given. For many parents the concept of I.Q. is mysterious. To give you a sense of what these tests measure, we will discuss the WISC III because it is used so often. It is divided into ten parts: five verbal and five performance. When evaluating the results of this test the psychologist is looking for overall potential to learn. The WISC III will yield three scores: Verbal I.Q., Performance I.Q., and Full-Scale I.Q. The average I.Q. score will fall between 90 and 110. But the score is not enough. You need to look at individual sub-test scores and think about how ADD might interfere with how well a child does. A child who is hyperactive will find it difficult to stay seated throughout the entire test (approximately one hour). Impulsive children may yell out the first thing on their mind and feel pressured to respond rapidly. And a child who is distracted may be more interested in the blocks or the puzzle parts or the questions to think about the right answer. Add to this the fact that most of the Performance Scales are timed, which can really throw some children with ADD. Only in consultation with other members of the team can the results make sense.

The Verbal Scale of the WISC III includes the following areas:

Information. This measures how much general information a child has learned from home and school.

Comprehension. This measures how well your child can think abstractly and understand concepts.

Similarities. This also measures a child's ability to think abstractly. Children are asked to tell how things are alike or different.

Arithmetic. This is not a paper-and-pencil arithmetic task. Rather, it measures mathematical reasoning skills. It does this by giving children problems to solve.

Vocabulary. Children are required to tell what a word means. A dictionary definition is not necessary, they can explain or define it.

Digit Span. This measures a child's ability to remember a sequence of numbers (forward and backward). This test is optional, it does not have to be given.

The Performance Scale of the WISC III includes the following areas:

Picture Completion. Children have to look at pictures and tell the examiner what part is missing.

Picture Arrangement. This requires a child to put pictures in order so that the story makes sense. It measures their ability to provide the whole when only parts are given.

Block Design. Unlike Picture Arrangement where children are given parts and make up the whole, this test measures a child's ability to look at the whole first, then break it into parts, then reconstruct the whole. It provides blocks and pictures and the child must put the blocks together to make the picture of the blocks.

Object Assembly. The child is given puzzle parts and must complete the puzzle. It measures a child's ability to make a whole out of its parts.

Coding. This section measures a child's ability to decipher a code and copy the correct symbols in a specific period of time.

Mazes. The child has to find the way out of a maze by using a pencil. Performance is also based on time.

In addition to measuring intelligence, the psychologist will look at behavioral and social-emotional functioning. She may use specific tests, interviewing techniques and/or rating scales. This enables her to rule out other psychological or psychiatric disorders that may be present, either with or without the attention deficit.

For a thorough list of assessment procedures see Barkley (1998).

8

~~~~~~

THE EDUCATIONAL EVALUATION

A thorough educational evaluation, sometimes referred to as a psychoeducational evaluation, will provide you with your child's educational strengths, weaknesses, and recommendations for educational interventions. Remember that a student's inability to stay on task, hyperactivity, distractibility, and/or impulsivity will affect her performance on the educational evaluation.

There is usually no certification or license for an educational evaluation. Therefore, parents need to be aware of the qualifications of the examiner. At very least, he should be a special educator who has a master's degree in special education from an accredited university. (In some states the school psychologist administers these tests.) He should have experience administering a battery of psychoeducational tests. He should be familiar with children with ADD and experienced in evaluating students when there is a suspicion of ADD. He should be willing to function as part of a team and to consult with other members of the team before, during, and after the evaluation. If he is reluctant to do so, find yourself another evaluator.

The educational evaluator must obtain information from a variety of sources in order to decide the most appropriate ways to evaluate the student's educational progress. Students with ADD typically do not do well on standardized tests. They often do better on individually administered tests because the examiner helps them to focus on the task. The fact that these tests are timed may cause stress and anxiety, which will also cause errors. Therefore, the tests may not truly represent what the child knows.

Beyond psychoeducational tests, information from parents about how their child does in school, what teachers report, how well she likes or dislikes school, how long it takes her to do homework, if she is easily distracted, and other descriptions of the child's behaviors will help to highlight the nature of the problem. After all, ADD is a complex disorder; the more information you can get from a wide variety of sources, the better able you are to examine the critical areas more thoroughly.

With this in mind, it is a priority to get information from the child's teachers: classroom teacher, special subject teachers (music, art, physical education, computer), lunchroom monitor, playground monitors, and others who come into contact with the child in the school setting. Sometimes school personnel are given rating scales to fill out, other times contacts can be made in person or on the phone. A rating scale is helpful in obtaining information from teachers (and parents) and should be viewed as an important part of the diagnostic process. A number of descriptions are listed and typically the teacher (or parent) is asked to check the appropriate rating (usually from 1 to 5, Always to Never) that best describes the child. Popular rating scales include the CGI-T: Conner's Global Index, the Snap Rating Scale, the Attention Deficit Disorders Evaluation Scale, and the Child Behavior Checklist. See the following for an example of a rating scale.

CGI-T: Conners' Global Index—Teacher
by C. Keith Conners, Ph.D.

Student's Name: _____ Gender: **M   F**
(Circle One)

Birthdate: ___/___/___   Age: _____   School Grade: _____
Month Day Year

Teacher's Name: _____ Today's Date: ___/___/___
Month Day Year

Instructions: Below are a number of common problems that children have in school. Please rate each item according to how much of a problem it has been in the last month. For each item, ask yourself, "How much of a problem has this been in the last month?", and circle the best answer for each one. If none, not at all, seldom, or very infrequently, you would circle 0. If very much true, or it occurs very often or frequently, you would circle 3. You would circle 1 or 2 for ratings in between. Please respond to all the items.

	NOT TRUE AT ALL (Never, Seldom)	JUST A LITTLE TRUE (Occasionally)	PRETTY MUCH TRUE (Often, Quite a Bit)	VERY MUCH TRUE (Very Often, Very Frequent)
1. Temper outbursts; explosive, unpredictable behavior	0	1	2	3
2. Excitable, impulsive	0	1	2	3
3. Restless or overactive	0	1	2	3
4. Cries often and easily	0	1	2	3
5. Inattentive, easily distracted	0	1	2	3
6. Fidgeting	0	1	2	3
7. Disturbs other children	0	1	2	3
8. Demands must be met immediately—easily frustrated	0	1	2	3
9. Fails to finish things he/she starts	0	1	2	3
10. Mood changes quickly and drastically	0	1	2	3

Once the evaluator has eliminated several or more areas of possible concern, she will use diagnostic tests in language, reading, writing, and math. These tests are more precise and enable the evaluator to pinpoint strengths and weaknesses. She will also evaluate how the child processes information—how are his perceptual skills, his memory skills, his thinking skills, his attention skills? Throughout this process the evaluator will obtain specific scores on tests. (See Key 31, Understanding Standardized Test Scores, for more information.) These test scores are important, but equally important is the information the examiner gleans by watching the child as he works on the tests. (How does the child approach tasks, process information, stay on task, deal with frustration, and respond to reinforcement?) A child may score well on a math test but throw his pencil down when he can't figure out an answer. A child may pay more attention to the sound of the air conditioner than to the spelling test. A child may answer questions very fast, then change the answer after he has a while to think about it. Observing how a child deals with the entire situation enables the evaluator to better understand how the child functions.

A thorough educational evaluation, which includes observation in the school setting, will establish the presence or absence of a learning disability. The child may have a learning disability that is causing him to appear to have an ADD. Or a child may have an ADD that is causing him to have academic problems that look like learning disabilities. Or they could exist simultaneously. (See Key 36.) The educational evaluator will also be able to look for other academic problems that may be causing the child to be hyperactive, distractible and/or impulsive, but not necessarily be ADD. When this information is shared and discussed with other professionals, a clearer picture of the nature of the child's disorder begins to appear.

9

THE SOCIAL HISTORY

The purpose of the social history is to look at the home and the family situation in order to obtain information that will be useful in diagnosing ADD. The social history should be taken by a social worker with an M.S.W. (Master of Social Work) from an accredited university. The social worker should be licensed and certified. (The criteria for certification differs from state to state.)

As all members of the multidisciplinary team do, the social worker should have experience with children with ADD and their families. A child or adolescent with ADD displays behaviors associated with ADD in both the school and home. To deal with the disorder only in the school may result in a misdiagnosis. The child must function at home, as a member of a family. There is no question that at some time all members of the family are affected by the child with ADD. To ignore the family would be foolhardy. Information about the family and how they function may lead to effective interventions.

Parents and other family members may be asked to fill out a questionnaire or respond verbally to questions from a social worker. You may find that you were asked some of these questions by the physician and/or the psychologist. The point is not to "trick" you. Rather, each professional is examining responses from his or her own professional perspective. The physician may not find a particular answer important, but the social worker may find that the same answer provides very useful information. The following information is typically sought in questionnaires:

- Where do you live?
- Does anybody besides your immediate family live with you?
- Do you own your own home or rent?
- What is your age?
- What is your occupation?
- How many years did you attend school?
- How is your health and that of other family members?
- Do you and your spouse have any marital problems?
- Length of pregnancy?
- Any problem with pregnancy and/or delivery?
- How does your child get along with siblings?
- Any family history of ADD or school-related problems?
- Do both parents agree on child-rearing techniques?
- What works well with your child? What doesn't?
- Are you easily frustrated by your child's behavior?
- How do you deal with this frustration?

This information provides a sense of how the family is functioning. For example, if grandparents live with the family, do they help out with child care or are they ill and dependent on other family members? If you live in an apartment building, do you feel pressured to control your child's behavior because the neighbors complain? If you live in a rural area, do you feel there is no one you can go to for support? Where you live and who lives there will give the social worker insight into the most effective interventions for your family.

Both parents should respond to questions on the social history, even if they don't live in the same household. Unless a parent is totally absent from the picture, the information from mother and father can provide the social worker with additional insight.

Together with the information gathered from the other evaluators, the multidisciplinary team will be able to get a picture of the total child, not just one aspect. This total view is critical because children who have attention deficit disorders display them at school, at home, on the playground, in the library, on the beach, and on the playing field—wherever they may be. It is not simply a school-related disorder.

For a social history to be useful, it must be thorough. A quick checklist simply won't provide the team with adequate information to make an informed decision. And although some of the questions will have been asked by other members of the team, they will be viewed through the eyes of a social worker. Together, all members of the team will discuss their findings and provide parents with a picture of the "total" child.

10

^^

COMORBIDITY

One of the more striking changes since the first edition of this book is the recognition that ADD can coexist with other disorders. In fact, a child diagnosed with ADD faces a significant risk for other disorders. Some experts say that risk may be as high as 65 percent.

The most frequently cited disorders are Learning Disabilities (see Key 36) and Oppositional Defiant Disorder (ODD), but there are others, such as mood disorders, conduct disorders, and Tourette syndrome.

According to the DSM IV, the essential feature of ODD is a recurrent pattern of negative, defiant, disobedient, and hostile behavior toward authority figures that persists for at least 6 months. These children are stubborn, don't take directions well, and can't compromise or negotiate. It appears they are always testing the limits. Most times this occurs in the home, but it may not occur in school or community. The diagnostic criteria* are listed below:

A. A pattern of negativistic, hostile, and defiant behavior lasting at least 6 months, during which four (or more) of the following are present:
   (1) often loses temper
   (2) often argues with adults

*From American Psychiatric Association: *Diagnostic and Statistical Manual of Mental Disorders*, Fourth Edition, Washington, DC, American Psychiatric Association, 1994.

(3) often actively defies or refuses to comply with adults' requests or rules
(4) often deliberately annoys people
(5) often blames others for his or her mistakes or misbehavior
(6) is often touchy or easily annoyed by others
(7) is often angry and resentful
(8) is often spiteful or vindictive

Note: Consider a criterion met only if the behavior occurs more frequently than is typically observed in individuals of comparable age and developmental level.

B. The disturbance in behavior causes clinically significant impairment in social, academic, or occupational functioning.
C. The behaviors do not occur exclusively during the course of a Psychotic or Mood Disorder.
D. Criteria are not met for Conduct Disorder, and, if the individual is age 18 years or older, criteria are not met for Antisocial Personality Disorder.

The causes of comorbidity are not clear. They may be genetic, environmental, or reactions to living with ADD suggests Thomas E. Brown, Ph.D., editor of *Attention Deficit Disorders and Comorbidities in Children, Adolescents, and Adults* and the Brown *Attention Deficit Disorders Scales*. What is clear is that parents and professionals need to be alerted to the fact that individuals with ADD may present other problems and the evaluation should be inclusive and thorough in order to assess the presence or absence of the other disorders.

11

~~~~~~

EVALUATING THE FINDINGS AND DRAWING CONCLUSIONS

Evaluating the findings is a team procedure and all the information gathered is important in making the diagnosis of ADD. Omission of any component may lead to a misdiagnosis and improper treatment.

Ideally, the team will meet in order to discuss the findings. Each member of the team will present his or her findings. This process allows all team members to have access to the best thinking on the child and to place the findings within the context of the child at home and at school. By not having access to information related to the family, the team might miss important aspects of the child's performance. And by the same token, not having a thorough educational evaluation may lead to an improper diagnosis.

A differential diagnosis will explore all possible causes for ADD. There are children who are hyperactive, impulsive, and distractible, but do not meet the criteria for ADD. Some of these children might be anxious or suffer from other emotional problems. Some may have undiagnosed learning disabilities.

The multidisciplinary approach may not always be possible. If that is the case, parents need to find out before they have any evaluation (1) that all the individual practitioners involved (physician, psychologist, special educator, and social worker) are willing to consult with each other before and during the evaluation process, (2) that the diagnosis of ADD or not having ADD will be a team decision, and (3) that the treatment plan will be developed and monitored by all professionals through frequent communications.

Professionals rely heavily on parents' reports with disorders affecting school and home. This is the case in the diagnosis of ADD. The parent interviews (medical, psychological, and social history) are necessary to eliminate other causal factors and to establish a basis for the diagnosis.

Good diagnosticians attempt to rule out other presenting problems and explore the frequency and duration of the attentional deficit. Parents who report that from day one their child slept little, was always fidgeting (i.e., thrashed his blankets around and moved from toy to toy) and "never paid attention" represents a different case from a child who was "fine" before entering school, and was referred by the teacher as being "hyperactive" because of a rough start in kindergarten and first grade. This child is also different from the child who has been doing well in school and at home, but because of a family crisis is referred by the school as being "distractible and impulsive."

Conclusions must be drawn based on all the facts. Frequently, the process of ruling out other disorders/disabilities leads to the diagnosis. Too many behaviors are described as ADD. This may lead not only to improper treatment for these students but also to a reduction of services for those students who truly are ADD. It minimizes the severity of this disorder to call any child who may be a little distractible or who cannot sit too long as having ADD. ADD is a specific diagnostic category that should be reserved for those students who meet the criteria proposed in the *DSM IV* and who have undergone a thorough, multidisciplinary evaluation. The diagnosis should be based on the criteria, the evaluation results, and the clinical expertise of the members of the evaluation team. This process will enable the team to develop a reasonable, sensible, and effective treatment plan based on the best information available.

Part Three

TREATMENT OF ADD

Any treatment plan must be multimodal, that is, medication when appropriate, behavior management techniques, interventions in the school, and counseling should be part of the plan. The following Keys will discuss these treatments.

12

^^^

MEDICATION

The use of medication to treat ADD is not new. In 1937, Dr. Charles Bradley prescribed Benzedrine, a stimulant, for children who were recovering from viral encephalitis, and found that it reduced their hyperactivity and distractibility.

The medications used today to treat ADD are effective and safe. Between 70 and 80 percent of children and adolescents treated with a stimulant show improvement—that is, children who have been properly diagnosed, not ones who are fidgety or a little distractible and whose pediatrician prescribes medication, or ones whose teacher suggests to their parents that they be "put on Ritalin" because they are very distractible. Only those children who have undergone a thorough multidisciplinary evaluation and are properly diagnosed as having ADD are candidates for medication. And not all of them need medication.

There are many myths associated with the use of medication with ADD. The foremost is that the stimulants have a paradoxical effect—that is, they calm students. Rather, stimulants increase the production of a neurotransmitter in the brain and bring it to acceptable levels, thereby increasing attention. They do not increase learning, they merely make the student more available for learning. And although the empirical research on the effectiveness of psychostimulants with children and adolescents with AD/HD is encouraging, this is not an easy decision for parents. Many parents feel guilty that they cannot solve their child's problems on their own; others will be criticized by friends and relatives for "putting" their child on "drugs." Still others will be so over-whelmed and confused that they cannot make a decision. Try to gather as much information as you can, and speak with a medical doctor you can trust—one who is competent, patient, and available.

Dr. Timothy E. Wilens, an Associate Professor of Psychiatry at Harvard Medical School and author of *Straight Talk About Psychiatric Medications for Kids*, provides a useful table on the types of medication for AD/HD. Generally, stimulants are the medication of choice, followed by antidepressants. Although many children and adolescents respond to stimulants, not all do. If there is no response, reevaluate the dose and consider another stimulant and other types of medication. Some of the common side effects of medication include loss of appetite, insomnia, depression, irritability, moodiness, and growth problems. Finally, when-ever a student is placed on medication there should be com-munication between the home and school. Parker's Medication Effects Rating scale is particularly effective for this purpose.

Medication Effects Rating Scale*

Name _____ Completed by _____

Date of Birth _____ Age ___ Sex ___ Grade ___

Date form completed _____

Medication(s)   Dosages and Times Administered Per Day

_____   _____

_____   _____

*From Parker, H. *The ADD-H Handbook for Schools*, Plantation, FL: Specialty Press, 1998.

Mark any changes noticed in the following behaviors:

Main Effects on Behavior	Worse	No difference	Improved a little	Improved a lot
Attention to task	____	____	____	____
Listening to lessons	____	____	____	____
Finishing assigned work	____	____	____	____
Impulsivity	____	____	____	____
Calling out in class	____	____	____	____
Organizing work	____	____	____	____
Overactivity	____	____	____	____
Restless, fidgety	____	____	____	____
Talkative	____	____	____	____
Aggressive	____	____	____	____
Peer interaction	____	____	____	____

Mark any side effects which you have noticed or which the child has mentioned.

Side Effects		Comments
_____	Appetite loss	_____
_____	Insomnia	_____
_____	Headaches	_____
_____	Stomachaches	_____
_____	Seems tired	_____
_____	Stares a lot	_____
_____	Irritability	_____
_____	Excessive crying	_____
_____	Motor or vocal tic	_____
_____	Nervousness	_____
_____	Sadness	_____
_____	Withdrawn	_____

13

▼▼▼

QUESTIONS ABOUT MEDICATION

The following are commonly asked questions concerning the medical management of children with ADD compiled by CHADD (Children and Adults with Attention Deficit Disorders) and the American Academy of Child and Adolescent Psychiatry.

What medications are prescribed for ADD children?

Medications can dramatically improve attention span and reduce hyperactive and impulsive behavior. Psychostimulants have been used to treat attentional deficits in children since the 1940s. Antidepressants, although used less frequently to treat ADD, have been shown to be quite effective for the management of this disorder in some children.

How do psychostimulants such as Dexedrine (dextroamphetamine), Ritalin (methylphenidate) and Cylert (pemoline) help?

Seventy to eighty percent of ADD children respond in a positive manner to psychostimulant medication. Exactly how these medicines work is not known. However, benefits for children can be quite significant and are most apparent when concentration is required. In classroom settings, on-task behavior and completion of assigned tasks is increased, socialization with peers and teacher is improved, and disruptive behaviors (talking out, demanding attention, getting out of seat, noncompliance with requests, breaking rules) are reduced.

The specific dose of medicine must be determined for each child. Generally, the higher the dose, the greater the effect and side effects. To ensure proper dosage, regular monitoring at different levels should be done. Since there are no clear guidelines as to how long a child should take medication, periodic trials off medication should be done to determine continued need. Behavioral rating scales, testing on continuous performance tasks, and the child's self-reports provide helpful but not infallible measures of progress.

Despite myths to the contrary, a positive response to stimulants is often found in adolescents with ADD; therefore, medication need not be discontinued as the child reaches adolescence if it is still needed.

What are common side effects of psychostimulant medications?

Reduction in appetite, loss of weight, and problems in falling asleep are the most common adverse effects. Children treated with stimulants may become irritable and more sensitive to criticism or rejection. Sadness and a tendency to cry are occasionally seen.

The unmasking or worsening of a tic disorder is an infrequent effect of stimulants. In some cases this involves Tourette's syndrome. Generally, except in Tourette's, the tics decrease or disappear with the discontinuation of the stimulant. Caution must be employed in medicating adolescents with stimulants if there are coexisting disorders, for example, depression, substance abuse, or conduct, tic, or mood disorders. In these cases medication may not be appropriate. Likewise, caution should be employed when a family history of a tic disorder exists.

One side effect, decreased spontaneity, is felt to be dose-related and can be alleviated by reduction of dosage or switching to another stimulant. Similarly, slowing of height and weight gain of children on stimulants has been documented, with a return to normal for both occurring upon discontinuation of the medication. Other less common side effects have been described but they may occur as frequently with a placebo as with active medication. Pemoline may cause impaired liver functioning in three percent of children, and this may not be completely reversed when this medication is discontinued.

Overmedication has been reported to cause impairment in cognitive functioning and alertness. Children may be attending to tasks, but their academic performance might suffer. Some children on higher doses of stimulants will experience what has been described as a *rebound effect*, consisting of changes in mood, irritability, and increases of the symptoms associated with their disorder. This occurs with varying degrees of severity during the late afternoon or evening, when the level of medicine in the blood falls. Thus an additional low dose of medicine in the late afternoon or a decrease of the noontime dose might be required.

When are tricyclic antidepressants such as Tofranil (imipramine), Norpramin (desipramine) and Elavil (amitriptyline) used to treat ADD children?
This group of medications is generally considered when contraindications to stimulants exist, when stimulants have not been effective or have resulted in unacceptable side effects, or when the antidepressant property is more critical to treatment than the decrease of inattentiveness. They are used much less frequently than the stimulants, seem to have a different mechanism of action, and may be somewhat less effective than the psychostimulants in treating ADD. Long-term use of the tricyclics has not been well studied. Children with ADD who are also experiencing anxiety or

depression may do best with an initial trial of a tricyclic anti-depressant followed, if needed, with a stimulant for the more classic ADD symptoms.

What are the side effects of tricyclic antidepressant medications?

Side effects include constipation and dry mouth. Symptomatic treatment with stool softeners and sugar free gum or candy are usually effective in alleviating the discomfort. Confusion, elevated blood pressure, possible precipitation of manic-like behavior and inducement of seizures are uncommon side effects. The latter three occur in vulnerable children who can generally be identified during the assessment phase.

What about ADD children who do not respond well to medication?

Some ADD children or adolescents will not respond satisfactorily to either the psychostimulant or tricyclic antidepressant medications. Nonresponders may have severe symptoms of ADD, may have other problems in addition to ADD, or may not be able to tolerate certain medications because of adverse side effects as noted above. In such cases, consultation with a child and adolescent psychiatrist may be helpful.

How often should medications be dispensed at school to an ADD child?

Since the duration for effective action for Ritalin and Dexedrine, the most commonly used psychostimulants, is only about four hours, a second dose during school is often required. Taking a second dose of medication at noontime enables the ADD child to focus effectively and to maintain appropriate school behavior and academic productivity. However, the noontime dose can sometimes be eliminated for children whose afternoon academic schedule does not require high levels of attentiveness. Some psychostimulants, Ritalin-SR (sustained release form) and Cylert, work for longer periods of time (eight to ten hours) and may help avoid the need for a noontime dose. Antidepressant medications used to treat ADD are usually taken in the morning, afternoon hours after school, or in the evening.

In many cases, the physician may recommend that medication be continued at nonschool times such as weekday afternoons, weekends or school vacations. During such nonschool times, lower doses of medication than those taken for school may be sufficient. It is important to remember that ADD is more than a school problem—it is a problem that often interferes in the learning of constructive social, peer, and sports activities.

How should medication be dispensed at school?

Because an ADD child may already feel different from others, care should be taken to provide discreet reminders to the child when it is time to take medication. It is important that school personnel treat the administration of medication in a sensitive manner, thereby safeguarding the privacy of the child or adolescent and avoiding any unnecessary embarrassment. Success in doing this will increase the student's compliance in taking medication.

The location for dispensing medication at school may vary depending upon the school's resources. In those schools with a full-time nurse, the infirmary would be the first choice. In those schools in which a nurse is not always available, other properly trained school personnel may take the responsibility of supervising and dispensing medication.

45

How should the effectiveness of medication and other treatments for the ADD child be monitored?

Important information needed to judge the effectiveness of medication usually comes from reports by the child's parents and teachers and should include information about the child's behavior and attentiveness, academic performance, social and emotional adjustment, and any medication side effects.

Reporting from these sources may be informal through telephone, or more objective via the completion of scales designed for this purpose. (See Key 8.)

The commonly used teacher rating scales are:

- CGI-T: Conners' Global Index-Teacher
- ADD-H Comprehensive Teacher Rating Scale
- Child Behavior Checklist
- ADHD Rating Scale
- Child Attention Problems (CAP) Rating Scale
- School Situations Questionnaire

Academic performance should be monitored by comparing classroom grades before and after treatment.

It is important to monitor changes in peer relationships, family functioning, social skills, capacity to enjoy leisure time, and self-esteem.

The parents, school nurse, or other school personnel responsible for dispensing or overseeing the medication trial should have regular contact by phone with the prescribing physician. Physician office visits of sufficient frequency to monitor treatment are critical in the overall care of children with ADD.

What are common myths associated with ADD medications?

Myth: Medication should be stopped when a child reaches teen years.

Fact: Research clearly shows that there is continued benefit to medication for those teens who meet criteria for diagnosis of ADD.

Myth: Children build up a tolerance to medication.

Fact: Although the dose of medication may need adjustment from time to time, there is no evidence that children build up a tolerance to medication.

Myth: Positive response to medication is confirmation of a diagnosis of ADD.

Fact: The fact that a child's attention span improves or activity levels decrease while taking ADD medication does not substantiate the diagnosis of ADD. Even some normal children will show a marked improvement in attentiveness when they take ADD medications.

Myth: Medication stunts growth.

Fact: ADD medications may cause an initial and mild slowing of growth, but over time the growth suppression effect is minimal or non-existent in most cases.

Myth: Taking ADD medications as a child makes you more reliant on drugs as an adult.

Fact: There is no evidence of increased medication taking when medicated ADD children become adults, nor is there evidence that ADD children become addicted to their medications.

Myth: ADD children who take medication attribute their success only to medication.

Fact: When self-esteem is encouraged, a child taking medication attributes his success not only to the medication but to himself as well.

14

CONTROVERSIAL
INTERVENTIONS

As a result of the increased interest in ADD over the years, there are a host of treatments that have been recommended to parents. Some have been demonstrated to be effective (medication when indicated, behavioral intervention, counseling, special education) while others are highly controversial. We will focus on three of the most popular treatments: diet, megavitamins, and biofeedback.

Diets

In 1975, Benjamin Feingold, M.D., published his best-selling book, *Why Your Child is Hyperactive*. His theory, based on his clinical observations as an allergist, was that food additives cause hyperactivity and learning disorders. His solution was simple—eliminate food additives. Dr. Feingold was a charismatic and powerful speaker and parents responded to him. It is also important to remember that at the time he proposed his diet many people were concerned about the food they ate and how it effected them. Before you knew it there were Feingold Associations cropping up through the United States. The diet listed below is an elimination diet. For many parents this was seen as a simple cure to ADD.

Group 1

Green pepper
Nectarines
Oranges
Plums and prunes
Peaches
Tangerines
All teas
Tomatoes

Group 2

Foods containing artificial flavors

Beverages
Candy
Chewing gum
Ice cream
Baked goods, except bread
Condiments
Gelatin
Preserves

Group 3

Foods containing artificial colors

Blues #1 and #2, Green #3, Reds #3 and #40, and Yellows #5 and #6. Two food colors are limited in use to one product each: Orange B for hot dogs and Citrus Red #2 for orange skin.

Group 4

Foods containing preservatives

Butylated hydroxy toluene (BHT)
Butylated hydroxy anisole (BHA)

Group 5
Foods containing natural salicylates

Almonds
Apples
Apricots
Cherries
Cloves
Coffee
Cucumber and pickles
Currants
Grapes and raisins

Although parents reported remarkable success with the diet, the scientific community responded with skepticism. Throughout the years since the diet was introduced there has been considerable debate over its effectiveness. Parents say it works, researchers say there is no support. Studies have been criticized for being poorly executed, and parents have been criticized for seeking quick cures. According to Silver, well-controlled studies have not found that food additives cause hyperactivity in 98 to 99 percent of the children. Why it works for the other 1 to 2 percent is not clear.

What about sugar? Parents often hear that sugar is the culprit that makes kids "hyper." Parents have told us that they know exactly when their child has had sugar because their behavior deteriorates rapidly. They are convinced that the sugar causes them to act more "hyper." What does the research say? In his book *Food and the Brain*, C. Keith Connors, Ph.D., says that there is no justification in the studies done so far to eliminate sugar from children's diets. He points to some interesting findings regarding sugar. For some children with ADD sugar can be helpful. Sugar can be either good or bad depending on a child's age, diet, and biology. He recommends that any change in diet should be made with the help of a nutritionist, dietitian, or physician who is knowledgeable in this area.

Megavitamins

In 1971, Dr. Alan Cott, a psychiatrist, suggested that large dosages of vitamins would reduce hyperactivity. These large dosages, at least ten times the recommended daily dosage, are referred to as "megavitamins." Once again parents wanted to try it and scientists were skeptical. In 1976, the American Academy of Pediatrics reported that there is no validity to the theory that megavitamins are useful in the treatment of hyperactivity or learning disabilities. There have been no studies reported that have changed that conclusion.

Biofeedback

Biofeedback has been used with children who have AD/HD in order to teach them to alter their brain wave pattern. By using an electroencephalogram (EEG), researchers have hypothesized that an altered brain wave pattern is associated with AD/HD. Once you learn to correct the pattern, AD/HD is improved.

This treatment is controversial, both from a theoretical and a treatment point of view. CHADD published a position paper on biofeedback in 1995 that advised parents not to use this treatment because of a lack of research to support it.

It is understandable why parents try these treatments. The problem is that such treatments tend to delay appropriate interventions and create false hopes for success. Proven interventions are time consuming. It may be hard to come to terms with the need for medication or the need for family counseling or the need to carry out a behavioral program in the home or the need for special education services. Any one of these decisions can be traumatic for parents. Yet the parent of a child with ADD may have to consider all of these. No wonder they are vulnerable to practitioners who propose a cure. We suggest that the first step in the process is to seek a multidisciplinary evaluation and soon thereafter to seek the support of parents who are having the same or similar experiences. There are groups throughout the United States who are supportive, knowledgeable, and generous with their time. You don't have to go through this alone. (See Appendix A, Resources for Parents.)

15

≈≈≈

BEHAVIORAL INTERVENTIONS

The use of principles and techniques of applied behavior analysis have been found to be very effective for behaviors associated with ADD. Although the term *applied behavior analysis* is often thought to be synonymous with behavior modification, it is not. We believe the use of the latter term has led to considerable confusion among parents. Many parents associate behavior modification with any procedure that changes behavior, such as shock treatment, psychosurgery, or extreme forms of punishment. It is also perceived as controlling and manipulative by many. Because the term has been inaccurately linked to these procedures in the minds of many, we prefer the term *applied behavioral analysis*.

The basic steps a parent carries out in a behavioral intervention may appear rather simple, but they are not. This Key will provide information about behavioral intervention that can be used with many children and adolescents with ADD. Additionally, some parents may need additional help from a professional trained in applied behavior analysis. Parents may also want to read one or more of the books listed below in that they are devoted entirely to this topic.

Becker, W.C. *Parents Are Teachers*. Champagne, Illinois: Research Press, 1971.

Hall, R.V. *Managing Behavior*, Parts 1, 2 and 3. Austin,

Texas: Pro-Ed Publications, 1972.

Paterson, G. *Living With Children*. Champagne, Illinois: Research Press, 1980.

Generally speaking, parents who use this approach attempt to arrange the environment of the home in such a way that specific consequences will increase behaviors (reinforcement) and specific consequences will decrease behaviors (punishment). They will do this in a systematic way so that they will be able to make decisions about which consequences are the most effective for the specific behaviors their child displays. (More detailed information will be provided in the Keys that follow.) Parents also learn to be more specific and objective when discussing their child's behavior and try to focus on the positive, not the negative. Parents often have questions about applied behavior analysis and we have listed the ones most frequently asked, with our responses.

Aren't you just bribing your child?

Technically, a bribe is defined as coercing something illegal or illicit. Obviously, we wouldn't condone either. What you are attempting to do is to motivate your child to engage in appropriate behaviors by providing reinforcement when she does so. (For example, "If you clean your room then you can watch TV") Also, you are not forcing your child to do anything. Rather, she has a choice. The reinforcement you employ should be so rewarding to her that she will engage in the appropriate behavior, but if she chooses not to, that's her right. It should also be noted that most of us work under a "reward" system in that we get paid for the work we do. And most important, there is considerable research that demonstrates that children are more enthusiastic about learning and learn more when their appropriate behaviors are reinforced.

Won't they want something every time they do the "right" thing?

Most of us receive something when we do the right thing, whether in pay, a bonus, a thank you, or a smile of appreciation. Some children find it very difficult to engage in appropriate behaviors; therefore, providing reinforcement for the appropriate behavior makes sense. Also, as the child begins to display appropriate behaviors, the behavior becomes a reward in and of itself. Over time, the child becomes less dependent upon the reward. Obviously, the timing will differ for each child.

This sounds a lot like the techniques you use to train animals, am I right?

You are right in that early research in this field was conducted in laboratories with animals. That is true for most research. The procedures employed with children and adolescents with ADD, however, have been studied in schools and homes for over the past four decades.

This seems like a lot of work, right?

Right again. Like anything done well, it takes time and planning, but parents of children and adolescents with ADD already spend considerable time dealing with inappropriate behaviors. When they employ these procedures they become more effective and gradually the appropriate behavior becomes second nature.

16

IDENTIFYING THE BEHAVIOR

The first step in the process of changing behavior is to identify the specific behavior you want to change. The goal should be a reasonable one and one that is not all encompassing. While it is understandable to want to eliminate all undesirable behavior and/or increase many desirable behaviors, the most prudent course appears to be to start small, learn the procedures, practice them with one or two behaviors, then expand. The behavior you are concerned about must be described in observable and measurable terms. You must be able to see it and count it. If we use general terms, such as hyperactive, impulsive, and distractible to describe a child's behavior, we run the risk of confusion. What exactly does hyperactive mean? How impulsive? What is distractible? All too often these terms mean different things to different people; hence, we are not able to understand exactly what the behavior is that we want to increase or decrease. It is not unusual, for example, for a husband and wife to disagree on the nature of the behavior.

By describing behaviors in precise terms, describing exactly what the child is doing and what we would like him to do, we avoid using emotionally-loaded, jargon-laden psychological terms. This has a marked advantage over other approaches in that the behavior can be readily described to all who may interact with the child—parents, babysitter, relatives, teachers, siblings, as well as the child. For example, rather than call a child "hyperactive," we could list the behaviors that are problemsome, such as jumping up and down, interrupting, being unable to sit still for more than a short period of time. These phrases are merely descriptions of behavior. They allow us to describe changes of behavior in clear, unambiguous terms. This also avoids the realization of a self-fulfilling prophecy whereby we categorize and classify our children's behavior and before long they live up to our label of them. (See the chart at the end of this Key for examples of changing a general, vague description of a behavior to a more precise, specific description.)

Trying to discover the rationale for behavior and trying to interpret behavior should be avoided. There may be ample justification for engaging in negative behavior, especially given the frustration experienced by children with ADD, but we still want to stop the negative behavior and replace it with a more appropriate behavior. For example, a child may shout an obscenity to a sibling because his toy is taken, and we may understand why he did it and empathize with his feelings of anger. But we also want to stop that socially undesirable behavior and teach the child to respond to similar situations in a different manner. It is difficult for some children to follow directions when there are other distractions (TV, videos, siblings talking), but we still want them to increase their ability to do so. By describing the behavior in precise terms, we can attempt to change it and evaluate how successful we are.

Probably the most effective way to become proficient in describing behavior precisely is to write the behavior on a piece of paper and share it with your spouse, a friend, or a neighbor. This process enables you to refine the definition of the behavior and make it more objective. When we are deeply involved in the lives of our children (as many of us tend to be), objectivity does not come easily. However, the more objective we can become and the more we begin to discuss behaviors rather than the child who is engaging in the behavior, the higher the probability of bringing about a change in negative behavior. The more often you apply this technique, the greater the probability that your role as parent will become a joy rather than a chore.

Identifying the Behavior

General, vague descriptions | *Precise, specific descriptions*

1. My daughter is lazy.
1. My daughter does not get out of bed when the alarm goes off.

2. Meals are a disaster with Jason.
2. During mealtime, Jason eats with his hands and hits his brother.

3. My son is very shy.
3. My son will not say "hello" when someone says "hello" to him.

4. Marion is an angry child.
4. Marion yells at her parents and sister.

5. He's terrible in the car
5. Whenever he is in the car, he refuses to put his seatbelt on and throws things out the window.

6. Alan is very negative.
6. Every time I ask him to do something, he says "no."

7. My kids never get along with each other.
7. When I come home from work, my son John tells me about the negative things his brother did to him.

8. My son has a lot of trouble going to bed.
8. John gets out of bed frequently and requests water.

9. If he doesn't get his own way, he throws a tantrum.

9. Whenever Ralph has to do something he does not like, he cries, lays on the floor, and kicks his legs.

10. My daughter is aggressive.

10. Sharon hits her younger brother if he takes her toys.

The more specifically you define the behavior, the better chance you have of changing it. Broadly defined behaviors are confusing to children and are difficult to measure.

17

REINFORCEMENT

Reinforcement is defined as anything that increases the strength of a behavior. If your child does something that pleases you and you praise her for it, she does it again. The more powerful the reinforcer the more likely the behavior will occur again. People respond to different types of reinforcers, for example, some of us respond to pay, others to food, and still others to a single "thank you." Nevertheless, there are some general guidelines that should be used when delivering reinforcement. The first thing you need to know is to start simply. The hierarchy of reinforcement is listed below.

1. Praise (verbal and nonverbal)
2. Praise coupled with activities
3. Praise coupled with tangible rewards
4. Token economy systems

Step one is to use praise. Too often parents think that reinforcement requires them to give their child expensive toys or gifts every time they do something appropriate. Although some types of tangible reward may be necessary for some children with ADD, one of the most effective ways to increase appropriate attending behavior is to praise (verbally and nonverbally) your child after she engages in appropriate behaviors.

Early research findings in this area provided parents with a simple dictum: "Catch them when they're good." It was clear that the more parents commented on their child's positive behavior, the more the child displayed the behavior. It sounds so simple, but it's not. Parents may be so attuned to focusing on negative behavior that they find the shift in focus very difficult. Some parents may find it awkward praising their children for appropriate behaviors. Some parents feel especially uncomfortable when praising their child outside of the home. Why, they wonder, do they have to praise desired behavior when other parents don't? And moreover, others look at them in disbelief. We offer no simple solutions other than it has been demonstrated to be effective. The professional literature and our experiences indicate that initially it is awkward and at times, uncomfortable to be so effusive in your praise. Yet, when you start receiving results it becomes worth it. A step-by-step guide to delivering praise is as follows:

1. Make a list of all appropriate behaviors your child engages in, no matter how simple they appear to be. Take nothing for granted. The easiest way to do this is to write down during a typical day every appropriate behavior from the time your child awakens until she goes to sleep. If both parents are available both should make lists. Do this independent of each other. You'd be surprised how much each of you miss.

2. Every time your child displays the targeted behavior say and/or do something positive. Try to vary your comments so that you are not continually saying "good." It's helpful if you can be specific in your praise. For example, "I like the way you got ready for school this morning, you really made me proud." Smiles, winks, and hugs should also be used frequently. If you feel you are unable to develop appropriate responses, see the following Key for suggestions.

3. Praise should be delivered only after your child displays the appropriate behavior. You are trying to establish a link between the behavior and the consequence. If you praise her when she is engaging in inappropriate behaviors you will increase them, which is exactly the opposite of what you are attempting to do.

4. Praise should be delivered very often in the beginning of a behavioral program. This continuous reinforcement serves to strengthen a behavior. As the behavior occurs more often, you can gradually reduce praise.

5. Praise should be delivered immediately after the behavior occurs in the beginning stages. Every time a positive behavior occurs, praise should be given. Over time you will be able to reduce the frequency of praise, but not until the behavior has been clearly established.

6. Praise should be genuine. Most parents we know are truly pleased when their child engages in appropriate behavior. Their praise merely reflects this. If you use praise in an artificial manner, children will see through it.

7. If you find it difficult to give praise try some of these tips:

   a. Post signs around the house (especially in the cupboards in the kitchen) to serve as reminders. (Example: Don't forget to let Adam know how much you appreciate his "eating behavior.")

   b. Tape record segments of the day and play it back in order to monitor your rate of praise.

   c. Buy a wrist golf counter and record your behavior each day. Try to increase it by ten percent daily.

   d. Put a piece of adhesive tape on your wrist and

make a mark each time you praise your child.

Praise will not be effective for every behavior associated with ADD. You may need to use additional reinforcers. What it will do, however, is reduce many minor disruptive behaviors and highlight those behaviors that may need additional reinforcement. Without this clarity every behavior takes on the same value. After a while physically abusing one's siblings becomes as important as not being ready when the school bus arrives. Even when praise alone is ineffective it should not be abandoned. You merely couple praise with the additional reinforcers noted above.

The next step in the hierarchy is praise coupled with activities. These activities should be ones readily available in your home; you should not have to go out and buy lavish rewards. Merely write down all the activities your child finds pleasurable. Every time they engage in the appropriate behavior have them "earn" the activity. These should be somewhat simple, such as being read to, watching TV, playing ball, playing a board game. Essentially children learn that first they do something that you want them to do, then they receive something they want.

Parents find this procedure to be very effective. You are not using threats ("Remember, if you want to play ball..."). Rather, you are allowing them to "earn" privileges when they engage in appropriate behaviors. Once again this may not be effective for all behaviors. If this does not work, proceed to the next step in the hierarchy.

Praise coupled with tangible reinforcement may be necessary for some children with ADD, especially younger children and those with more severe deficits. As noted above, praise should be continued and coupled with a tangible reinforcement immediately after the behavior occurs. Try to think of all the tangible rewards your child likes. These can be stickers, pencils, pads, food, or any small item your child enjoys. Use only small amounts. Try to spread the rewards throughout the day. In many cases parents benefit from consultation with a professional well versed in applied behavior analysis techniques at this point. The use of tangibles needs to be closely monitored.

It may also be appropriate to implement a *token economy system*, that is, a system whereby you child earns points, stars, tokens, and similar items that can be traded in at a later date for specified reinforcements. Some children and adolescents benefit from the use of contracts, that is, when a parent and child develop an agreement specifying what each must do. These contracts are not impossible to carry out on your own, but we believe it is wise to consult a professional. Once you are able to develop the skills necessary to carry out such programs the quicker you will see changes in your child's behavior. And you are more apt to develop such skills under the guidance of a professional.

18

SELECTING
REINFORCERS

Some parents may have a hard time coming up with potential reinforcers for their children. Below is a list developed by Dr. R.Vance Hall of the University of Kansas that we have modified. While it is not exhaustive, it does provide parents with a good start.

Potential Reinforcers for Preschoolers

Social Reinforcers

Verbal
1. Specific praise.
2. Indirect praise (telling someone else how good they are).
3. Suggested words or phrases: "Yes." "Great." "That's right." "That's fine." "Good." "Uh-huh." "Keep going." "O.K." "All right." "Pretty." "Doing better." "I like that." "Good job." "I'm pleased." "I'm proud of you." "Show us how." "You're polite." "Thank you." "I'm glad to see you." "It makes me happy when you…." "I like the way you…." "Do that again for me."

Physical
Hugs. Kisses. Smiles. Eye contact. Tickle. Wink. Handshake. Touch. Toss into the air or whirl around. Piggyback ride. Pat on the back. Chuckling/cheering. Jumping up and down. Tweaking nose.

Material Reinforcers

Toys/balloons. Books/puzzles/magazines. Snacks of favorite food. Pennies for bank.

Activity Reinforcers

Trip to park, zoo, library (any special outing). Going to work with Dad or Mom. Play with friends. Listening to stories or songs/singing songs. Play on swingset or in sandbox. Spending the night with Grandma/Grandpa or favorite adult. Opportunity to feed pet. Rocking. Playing a game/playing catch with parent/having a friend over to play or eat. Finger play. Take a picture of how good they are while they are (a) sitting on a potty, (b) displaying good table manners, (c) going to bed. Talking into a tape recorder/listening to records. Going out for a meal, snack, or movie. Playing with dough or clay. Finger painting/coloring. Blowing bubbles. Helping mom or dad. Longer time in bathtub or not having to take a bath (also bubble bath). Ride in car or on bicycle with adult/riding tricycle. Extended bedtime-skip nap. Watching TV. Going outside (day or night). Help hold baby/help give baby a bath. Swimming/being pulled in a wagon/swinging. Carry purse or attache case for adult. Display of art work. Playing with toys. Using telephone to tell of success. Special ride on escalator or elevator. Helping cook a meal or choosing the menu. Help water grass, flowers, or plant a garden. Camping out in the backyard.

Token Reinforcers

Stars on a chart, backed by material and activity reinforcers listed above.

Potential Reinforcers for Elementary Children (Ages 5–11) at Home

Social Reinforcers

Verbal

1. Specific praise.
2. Indirect praise (telling someone else about what they did or accomplished).
3. Suggested words and phrases: "Yes." "O.K.!" "Neat." "Good." "Great." "Delightful." "Brilliant." "Swell." "Fine answer." "That's right." "Beautiful." "Exciting." "Positively." "Go ahead." "Yeah." "All right." "Correct." "Marvelous." "Nifty." "Excellent." "Perfect." "How true." "Absolutely." "Exactly." "Cool." "Outstanding." "Go on." "Good response." "Wonderful job." "Fantastic." "Absolutely." "Of course!" "Fabulous." "That's clever." "I'm pleased." "Thank you." "I'm glad you're here." "It makes me happy when you...." "You perform well...." "I'm so proud of you for...." "You do so well at...." "We think a lot of you when...." "That put you tops on our list." "That shows a great deal of work." "That's a nice expression." "That's interesting." "That was very thoughtful." "Show me how to do that." "You're doing better." "I like that." "This is the best yet." "You were polite to..." "No one could have done it better." "Let's put this somewhere special." "Show this to your father/mother."

Physical

Hugs/squeeze. Kisses. Handshake. Wink. "O.K." gesture with thumb. Pat on the back. A teasing gesture. Eye contact.

Material Reinforcers

Toys. Tricycle. Bicycle. Pets. Books. Games. Puzzles. Food.

Own bedroom. Clothing. Musical Instruments. Skates/skate-board. CDs. Own TV-Radio-Stereo. Personal items such as hair dryer, own telephone.

Activity Reinforcers

Playing game with parent. Spending time with parent. Special outing. Play with friends. Reading or being read to. Overnight with relative or friend. Decorating room or home for special event. Helping parent (cook, work in yard, sew or construct something). Feed the baby. Extended bedtime. Shopping. Eating out. Plan a day's activities. Watching TV or listening to records. Freedom from chores. Using the telephone. Planting a garden. Taking special lessons (such as music, athletics, art). Public display of work. Party for friends. Going to hamburger stand.

Token Reinforcers (backed by reinforcers listed above)

Stars on a chart. Points. Poker chips. Allowance. Own bank account.

Material Reinforcers

Food. Choice of seat in room. Special pencil or pen. Balls, jump ropes, other playground equipment.

Potential Reinforcers for Junior High Youths (Ages 12–14) at Home

Social Reinforcers

Verbal
1. Specific praise.
2. Kidding and joking.
3. Suggested words or phrases: "Neat." "Fantastic." "Wow." "Super." "Great." "Nice." "On a scale of 1 to 10, you are an 11!" "It is a pleasure having you as a...

(son or daughter)." "I'm proud of you." "I like your attitude (behavior)." "That was very thoughtful." "You just made my life easier." "You are a lot of help." "You do so well at..." "It pleases me when you..." "I like that outfit." "That's so-o-o good." "Show us how to do that." "That's better."

Physical

Smiles. Eye contact. Physical contact (only if adolescent approves). Winks.

Material Reinforcers

Favorite meal. Snack. Clothes. Books and magazines. Own phone-TV-radio. Stereo. Tapes. C.D.'s. Moped. Electric razor. Hair dryer. Curlers. Own room. Gift certificate. Guitar or other musical instruments. Money. Sports equipment. Hobby items. Own pet.

Activity Reinforcers

Participate in activities with friends. Special lessons (such as music, sports, modeling, art). Roller skating. Additional time on telephone. Playing stereo. Choosing own bedtime. Extended curfew. Staying up late. Staying overnight with friends. Time off from assigned chores. Opportunity to earn money. TV privileges. Being chairperson of a family meeting. Decorating own room. Camping out. Summer camp. Expensive haircut. Trip to amusement park. Sleeping late. Discussion with parents. School activities. Party for friends. Taking a friend out for pizza. Shopping trip (clothes). Ski trip. Bowling. Sporting events. Time with parents alone (apart from younger brothers and sisters).

Token Reinforcers

Points (backed by any reinforcer above). Money.

Potential Reinforcers for Senior High Youths (Ages 15–18) at Home

Social Reinforcers

Verbal

1. Specific praise.
2. Kidding and joking.
3. Indirect praise (telling someone else about what they did or accomplished).
4. Suggested words or phrases: "Swell." "All right." "Super." "Great." "Bravo." "Well done." "Commendable." "Delightful." "Excellent." "Likeable." "Terrific." "How true." "Good job." "That's clever." "I'm pleased." "I'm glad you're here." "That's a prize of a job." "It makes me happy when you..." "Lookin' good." "Yeah." "How beautiful." "Well thought out." "You are very sincere." "That shows thought." "This is the best yet." "Now you're really trying." "You have a good attitude." "Keep up the good work." "Your room looks so neat." "Whatever you decide is okay." "That was a good suggestion." "What is your opinion?" "What would you suggest?"

Physical

Smiles. Eye contact. Nods. Physical contact (only if adolescent approves).

Material Reinforcers

Books. Pets. Playing cards. Games. Musical instruments. Records. Tapes. Sports equipment. Tools to work on car or motorcycle. Typewriter, record player, TV. Own telephone. Clothes. Electrical equipment (for example, shaver, hair dryer, make-up mirror). Craft kits. Favorite food. Car keys. Money.

Activity Reinforcers

Leading family groups. Exempting a duty or assigned task. Cooking. Working on car or cycle. Listening to TV, stereo, tapes. Talking on the telephone. Free time with peer group. Special outing (parent pays) such as, musical group, sporting event, bowling, roller/ice skating, movie. Remodeling, redecorating room. Shopping trip. Friend staying overnight or staying with friend.

Token Reinforcers

Points (appropriate for some 14- to 15-year-olds, backed by material and/or activity reinforcers). Money.

The Reinforcement Questionnaire that follows is helpful with selecting reinforcers.

REINFORCEMENT QUESTIONNAIRE

Name: _____ Date:_____

School: _____ Age:_____

Filled out by: _____

1. The things I like to do most after school are _____

2. If I had $10, I'd _____

3. My favorite TV programs are _____

4. My favorite game at school is _____

5. My best friends are _____

6. My favorite time of day is _____
   because _____

7. My favorite toys are _____

8. My favorite record or tapes are _____

9. My favorite subject at school is _____

10. I like to read books about _____

11. The places I'd like to go in town are _____

12. My favorite foods are _____

13. My favorite inside activities are _____

14. My favorite outside activities are _____

15. My hobbies are _____

16. My favorite animals are _____

17. The three things I like to do most are _____

_____

_____

_____

18. The three I would like to have most are _____

_____

_____

_____

19. The three things I like to do *least* are _____

_____

_____

_____

19

~~~~~~

PUNISHMENT

Reinforcement does not always work. There are times when a negative consequence needs to be applied in order to change a behavior. And in many cases the combination of high rates of reinforcement and low rates of punishment may be the most effective solution of all.

According to applied behavior analysts, anything that decreases a behavior is defined as a *punisher*. This does not include any form of physical punishment, usually known as corporal punishment. Spanking or hitting any child or adolescent is wrong for a number of reasons. To intentionally inflict physical harm on another human being is inexcusable. The message to children is clear that those bigger and stronger and more powerful than you can get you to do what they want by force. It is not surprising that children and adolescents then choose this as a strategy for dealing with others. From a behavioral point of view, spanking and hitting are ineffective and teach our children and adolescents the wrong behavior. Children and adolescents learn from our behavior; we must demonstrate civilized ways of dealing with conflict if we are to be appropriate role models.

It is difficult dealing with inappropriate behaviors that occur frequently day in and day out. However, there are effective alternative methods available to parents. If you feel you are in danger of employing corporal punishment with your child, we suggest you seek help to resolve this problem.

As there is with reinforcement, there is a hierarchy in

the use of punishment. Too often parents escalate their response rapidly and go from telling a child to "stop that!" to sending him to his room for an interminable period of time. There are several intermediate steps:

1. Ignore inappropriate behaviors
2. Verbal reprimands
3. Removal of privileges
4. Time-out

Parents are often told to "ignore it and it will go away." It's not so simple. *Ignoring inappropriate behaviors* is a very effective technique, but one that many parents find difficult to implement. The technical phrase used to describe ignoring is "time-out from social reinforcement." The idea is that there is reinforcement occurring in the child's environment and the absence of this reinforcement (ignoring) will encourage the child to engage in the appropriate behavior to receive reinforcement. This process is also hard to carry out. Parents are often frustrated by their inability to ignore inappropriate behaviors. Here are a few suggestions:

1. Never stand there staring at your child while he engages in the behavior.
2. Go to another room.
3. Listen to music. A walkman is helpful.
4. Keep busy—cook, read, and so forth.
5. Use "self talk." Tell yourself that the behavior will pass and this is an effective procedure.
6. Husbands and wives should assist each other as they ignore inappropriate behaviors.

Don't be surprised if the behavior increases at first. Think about it. How many times have you not paid attention to (ignoring) a behavior, but it finally got to you and you responded. Your child asks you for a cookie before dinner, you say "no." He continues to ask, the requests now becoming incessant. Finally, you scream, "Take the cookie and let me finish making dinner!" It's easy to do, we've done it more than a few times. Unfortunately, that only teaches kids that the longer they persist and the more annoying they can become, the more likely you will give in to their request. So it's not surprising that in the initial stages of ignoring, your child will continue to pursue the previously learned strategy. Just try to sustain the ignoring until you see a change in behavior. Do not ignore behaviors that are injurious to your child or anybody else, or destructive to property however.

Ignoring is most effective when used in combination with reinforcement of the desired behavior. Your child should get your attention when engaging in desirable, not undesirable, behavior.

Ignoring is hard and may take a long time to decrease a behavior. Also, it is probably the most effective for behaviors that are reinforced by verbal and nonverbal praise. Because it is hard to ignore behaviors, this technique is often not employed to its maximum usefulness. On the other hand, there are many behaviors that will not be changed merely by systematically ignoring them and you may have to proceed to Step 2 (verbal reprimands).

Verbal reprimands should be kept small and to the point. Too much discussion of the inappropriate behavior may only serve to increase or maintain it. For example, the reasons why the child should not engage in the behavior, its effect on you, on the child, or on other members of the household, and so forth, will not be understood. Rather than saying, "I must have told you one thousand times not to interrupt me when I'm using the food processor. Don't you realize I could get hurt? Can't you just wait like everyone else? I'll never get this done if you keep interrupting me," a simple "no," "enough," "stop," "please don't do that" will suffice. Once the child engages in the appropriate behavior, reinforce her.

Many times verbal reprimands go unheeded and you need to move to Step 3, *removal of privileges*. This is not done in haste ("That's it, you're not leaving the house today" or "Forget about going to the beach tomorrow"). It should be carried out in a well-thought-out manner, and the ground rules should be discussed with your child. She should know that if she engages in a specified behavior she will not get certain rewards. The underlying principle is that children are always earning reinforcements; when they display certain undesirable behaviors these reinforcements are unattainable. This procedure can be used with verbal reprimands if necessary.

If all of the above steps fail to decrease inappropriate behaviors, you may need to employ other more complex procedures. These are best undertaken with the advice of a professional trained in applied behavior analysis. The program must be developed, implemented, and monitored in a systematic fashion.

There are a few cautions about the use of punishment. According to the professional literature, most interaction between parent and child is negative. That is, parents tend to comment much more on the negative behaviors that their children engage in than the positive behaviors. Therefore, punishment must be used sparingly and with high rates of verbal and nonverbal praise and other reinforcements. If delivered out of frustration and anger and employed excessively; punishment will not change behaviors.

20

SETTING LIMITS

Clearly established limits are helpful for all of us. They help define the parameters of acceptable and unacceptable behavior. When limits are set in a fair and reasonable manner, they allow us to know exactly what is expected of us. This is especially true for children with ADD. When limits are set, children and adolescents with ADD do not have to guess what the rules of the game are because they are presented to them in a clear manner that is explicitly stated. One way to do this is to set up rules for your home. When making rules try to:

1. Make them as positive as possible.
2. Make them specific.
3. Make as few as possible.
4. Make the link between rules and consequences specific.

The first guideline is to *make the rules as positive as you possibly can*. The rationale is that you want to specify what appropriate behaviors are expected. It's far better to say, "You are to come to the dinner table no more than five minutes after you hear the timer" than "Don't be late for meals." This type of statement also makes it easier to deliver reinforcement because it serves as a reminder, that is, Jim followed the rules, therefore he should receive some kind of reinforcement. It's not always easy to give this kind of reinforcement, but you should make an attempt. One suggestion is to try to think of all the things your child must do to follow the rule. This process should help you state these steps, which then become rules, in a positive fashion.

Second, *make the rules specific*. This allows for little interpretation. For example, "No fighting with your brother" may lead to a lengthy discussion over what is "fighting" and what isn't "fighting." By specifying the rules clearly you insure better compliance. Rules that are too general are difficult to follow because you are not really sure what the rule is. We have seen rules such as "act appropriately." This statement is simply too broad and leads to a variety of interpretations.

The third guideline is to *use as few rules as you can*. Too many rules are confusing and difficult to follow. Select those behaviors that are the most problematic and establish rules for them. Many parents will have rules for getting ready for school, eating, and bedtime. You may have more, but your rules will never cover every possible behavior your child engages in. Make a rule only if it is necessary. Periodically sit down with your child and revise the rules if applicable.

Finally, *be sure the consequences of behavior, either contrary to or in accordance with the rules, are explicit*. It is a good idea to write the rules on a piece of oaktag and list the consequences, most of which will be positive. Some parents use photographs of their child engaging in the appropriate behavior and post them next to the rules to encourage compliance. It's also very reinforcing for the child when others see these pictures. Whenever your child follows the rules, recognize and reinforce it. Depending upon the nature of the behavior, verbal praise may be sufficient or you may want to use a more tangible reward.

In addition to establishing rules, you may want to use the behavioral principle of contingency in setting limits. Contingent reinforcement is a powerful tool. Essentially you require your child to do something to receive something. You are establishing a link between behavior and reward. Some examples: "First you clean your room, then you can have an ice cream cone"; "Get dressed, then you can have breakfast"; "Do your homework, then you can watch TV," and so on. This allows your child to know exactly what is required in order to receive the reinforcement. Then your child has the free will to choose what to do. What you attempt to do is to make the reinforcement so powerful it becomes an irresistible offer. As with most interventions, there are a few guidelines that will assist you in successful implementation:

1. Start with small increments of behavior.
2. Make the contingency meaningful.
3. Make sure the contingency is reinforcing.

Initially you *start small*. You wouldn't want to say, "If you do well on your report card, we'll go out for dinner." This may be fine in addition to other contingencies or at a later stage, but not now. Now you want to keep it short and simple: First you do this, then you get that; for example, clean room—watch TV, set table—special dessert. In all instances, the model is first do something you don't like, then you get something you do like.

If possible, try to *make the contingency meaningful*. If you want your child to clean her room and she goes to the room to watch TV, then use TV as an reinforcer contingent upon room cleaning. If your child dawdles in the morning and watches TV, make TV watching contingent upon getting dressed first.

Finally, *make sure the contingency is rewarding*. For example, you say to your child, "First get dressed, then you can have breakfast." This is fine if breakfast is valued by your child, but if he couldn't care less if he ate breakfast, then it won't work.

The establishment of rules and the use of contingencies are helpful in letting your child know exactly what you expect. The more they know what to expect, the more likely they will meet the expectation. The guesswork is taken out of parental requests and demands, and the stage is set for more effective management of behavior.

21

~~~~~~

THE NEED FOR STRUCTURE, CONSISTENCY, AND PREDICTABILITY

Effective school programs for children with ADD provide a great deal of *structure*. Structure does not imply rigidity. Rather a structured approach is one in which students know exactly what is expected of them, which behaviors are acceptable and unacceptable, what the consequences are for each behavior, and what the time frame is for each expected behavior. For example, a schedule is usually written on the board so that students will know exactly what will occur at what time. Routines are established early in the year and followed on a daily basis. There are times when events occur that deviate from these schedules and students may have a hard time. Over time, however, they become more able to deal with the changes. A structured approach allows for teachers and students to be consistent, and it is this consistency that allows for predictability. Students with ADD benefit greatly from this concept because they don't have to think about the extraneous things that go on in a school day. They can focus their energies on relevant aspects of instruction.

Despite a parent's best effort, it is difficult and probably not advisable to try to duplicate the school situation at home. It is important to recognize, however, that the transition from a structured approach at school to an unstructured one at home can lead to problems. What should parents do? Parents can bridge the gap by providing a modicum of structure in the home, especially on weekends and holidays. Many parents of children with ADD recognize the need to stick to daily routines during the week (for example, come home from school, have a snack, do homework, relax, eat, watch TV, go to bed), but abandon these routines on weekends and holidays. For many children with ADD, it is during these loose periods of time that they experience difficulty. Establish some kind of schedule on weekends. Initially try not to deviate from the routines you establish. Begin with small blocks of time, such as:

8:30	Breakfast
9:00	Chores in room/house
10:30	Go to park
12:00	Lunch
1:00	Library
3:30	Free time
5:00	Help with dinner preparation
6:00	Dinner
7:00	Bath and free time
8:30	Bedtime

Obviously, the schedule will vary tremendously for each child or adolescent, depending on his age and grade, the severity of the disorder, and his interests. The idea is to create some structure by having and adhering to a schedule. Gradually you can expand the blocks of time to morning, afternoon, and evening, and you and your child can fill in activities that you will do during these times. When children are easily distracted by the environment around them, the structure you provide can bring about a sense of order in a chaotic world. Talk to your child's teacher to see if he can assist you in developing a meaningful schedule over long vacations, especially the summer.

Structure also implies a certain amount of organization. Clothes, objects, school items, and so forth, should be stored in the same place. You can start by organizing your child's room so that she knows exactly where things are located. Try to involve her in this. Clothes should be selected for school by the child the night before, items necessary for school (lunch, books, papers) should be placed on the table near the door, and important items such as house keys should be kept in the same place every day, such as a basket by the door. Keeping track of these things may seem minor, but all together they lessen the number of things your child has to think about.

Children and adolescents with ADD also benefit from *consistency*, not only in the manner in which you deal with them, but also, in the case of a two-parent household, in the manner in which parents deal with each other. This is where family rules will be helpful. It is important that specific consequences always occur for specific behaviors, that rules are uniformly adhered to, and that there is agreement on these issues by both parents. When parents disagree on child rearing techniques, they are doomed to failure. Children are masters of "divide and conquer" and will readily recognize opportunities to benefit from such a division. If your son or daughter knows that homework comes before watching TV, and that both mother and father will enforce and reinforce such a rule, they will not attempt to negotiate. You may not agree on everything, but major child rearing practices should be agreed on for the benefit of your child. At the very least, do not disagree in the presence of your child. If you have marked differences of opinion, seek professional assistance in order to work out the problems. It has been our experience that unless this is done, the lack of consistency will only serve to exacerbate hyperactive, distractible, and impulsive behaviors in both children and adolescents.

This also applies to families where parents share the custody of the child. As much as possible, both households should strive to provide consistent, predictable expectations and consequences for the child. We recognize that this may be difficult, but it is very important to your child. We know of parents who have sought the help of a professional to assist them in ironing out a reasonable approach to setting consistent limits in both households.

Finally, there is a need for *predictability*. For children and adolescents with ADD, much of the world appears to function in an unpredictable manner. By providing structure and consistency, you will become more predictable to your child. He will know exactly how you will respond to specific situations. We have asked many children with ADD the following questions:

• When you act appropriately, what do your parents do?
• When you act inappropriately, what do your parents do?

Although some children can tell you what occurs when they act inappropriately, the overwhelming number of these children are at a loss to describe the link between their behavior and the response of their parents. In their minds, their parents' responses occur by chance, depending on their moods. If children and adolescents fail to recognize a link between behavior and consequences, that is, between their behavior and their parents' response, they will have a very difficult, if not impossible, time engaging in appropriate behavior. Try this with your child. Role play a situation where you and your child reverse roles (you play them and they play you). See how they respond; observe the way in which they act like you act; look for consistency. If your child can mimic you to a certain extent, you are probably fairly predictable. If she appears to be lost, you need to establish a more consistent, predictable manner. The more predictable you become, the more your child will be able to respond appropriately to the world around her. You may know people who are unpredictable; you never know how they will respond to a situation. Many people find this disconcerting. Couple this with ADD and you have a situation that can only lead to failure.

A structured, consistent, predictable environment will provide children with ADD with a sense of confidence and security. They know that there is a great deal of disarray around them, but at the very least, their home is a haven. And remember, they won't always agree with your actions, but at least they will know what your actions will be.

22

^^^

SOCIAL SKILLS TRAINING

Many children with ADD have social skills deficits. They need to learn how to act appropriately, how to establish relations with their peers, teachers, and family. Moreover, as individuals move from childhood through adolescence to adulthood, this is critical for their success. *What are social skills?* The ability to understand how your behavior affects others is a social skill. Knowing how to make friends is a social skill. Knowing when and where to say certain things is a social skill. Many children with ADD are unaware of the effect of their behavior on others. They may say the wrong thing at the wrong time or have difficulty making friends. Parents readily identify such deficiencies.

Over the past twenty years a number of professionals have addressed this issue and developed social skills training programs. These programs attempt to make children aware of their own behavior and to teach them how to act in socially appropriate ways. You should find out if your school has social skills groups or if there are groups run by professionals in the community. If your child is receiving special education services, social skills training should be included in the I.E.P. (Individualized Education Program).

As a parent you can also teach these skills to your child with the proper instruction from a professional. And while parents bemoan the fact that these skills have to be taught, it has been our experience that many parents of children with ADD recognize that their children have to be explicitly taught many things that others pick up incidentally. Parents can follow five basic components of social skills training suggested by Cartledge and Milburn in their book, *Teaching Social Skills to Children and Youth*:

1. Provide instruction.
2. Present a model.
3. Rehearse.
4. Provide feedback.
5. Practice.

Provide Instruction

Parents must be as explicit as possible when describing the social skills they want their child to develop. Too often children and adolescents know what they are not supposed to do, but are vague when it comes to things they should be doing. Part of the reason for this behavior is lack of training. As parents, we assume our children know what we are talking about. However, for many children and adolescents with ADD we cannot make such assumptions. Social skills training forces us to identify exactly what the components of appropriate social behavior are and to describe them in a clear, unambiguous manner to our children. Let's take mealtime as an example. This tends to be a difficult time for many parents of children with ADD. Parents have very specific expectations and feelings about how a family should behave during this time. Unfortunately, this is frequently at odds with the behavior of the child with ADD. In order to reduce this discrepancy, identify a few behaviors that you could provide instructions to your child. You should start small, for example:

1. Come to the table within five minutes from the time I call you. (Set a kitchen timer with a loud bell.)
2. Sit in your chair.
3. Use appropriate eating utensils.
4. Remain in your chair throughout the meal.

At this point in the training a brief discussion of each behavior is sufficient. These are your expectations. Don't overload your child with too much information. Some parents find it helpful to list these skills on a chart to be kept in a visible space in the kitchen.

Present a Model

A model is a demonstration of the desired behavior. At first you demonstrate and your child copies your behavior. Keep it simple. In the case of mealtime behavior, you can act out exactly how you would like your child to come to the table, sit, eat appropriately, and remain seated. Depending upon the severity of the ADD and/or the child's age, you may start with only one behavior, then move on when the behavior is mastered. After you demonstrate the behavior, you should attempt to use different models. Some parents have been very successful with puppets, pictures, photographs, TV, videos, and books. Try to find anything that allows you to provide examples of the social skill you are teaching. When selecting a model make sure that the most important element clearly demonstrates the skill you are teaching. One of the difficulties encountered by children with ADD is the inability to discriminate between relevant and irrelevant information. If there are a lot of distractors, your child might focus on these, and not on the skill you are teaching. Generally speaking, the more models you provide, the higher probability learning will take place.

Rehearse

By rehearsing social skills children are able to act out and practice the newly developed skill in a controlled environment. For children with ADD, the most effective type of rehearsal is verbal and motor responding. Talk through each step of the skill and allow the child to perform it. Role playing can also be employed at this stage. However, role playing has to be carefully orchestrated for children with ADD; otherwise, it will be a useless activity. It is more than you playing a role with your child. You should clearly specify what behaviors they are to perform and when they should perform them. Many children respond favorably to role playing if it is carried out with this kind of specificity.

Provide Feedback

Without information about their performance, most children with ADD won't know how they did. This feedback is critical to the success of a social skills training program. Objective, nonevaluative feedback should be given for each task performed. Tell them what they did without criticism. Feedback can be corrective ("when you sit at the table, please try not to bump into your brother") and/or reinforcing ("you've been great at getting to dinner on time"). Some children benefit from video and audiotape feedback of their performance. They may perceive this as more objective than a parent. This is especially true for adolescents with ADD, for many find it difficult to accept feedback from an adult but respond beautifully when they listen to a tape of their performance or view a video.

Practice

Once your child has performed the behavior alone, that is, without any assistance from you, she is ready to practice it under different conditions. In the beginning stages parents should provide continuous reinforcement to ensure that the skill is learned. You may find that there are "slip-ups." Merely go back to the step necessary to ensure success.

The five-step procedure is extremely useful for parents of children with ADD. It provides a strategy for dealing with problematic behaviors in a reasonable manner. Children respond very positively because they are not being berated for their behavior but are being taught to engage in appropriate social skills. They also like it because they are receiving reinforcement at every step. See Appendix A, Resources for Parents, for a list of social skills training programs.

23

~~~~~~

INCREASING SELF-ESTEEM

The term *self-esteem* is certainly one of the most overused words in education and psychology. It seems that almost every personal or school failure is laid at the doorsteps of "low self-esteem." Unfortunately, this has caused many to downplay the importance of our feelings about ourselves. There is considerable evidence in the professional literature regarding the relationship between our feelings about how we will perform and how we actually perform. Many students with school problems do not feel they are capable of success; therefore, they don't try. At an early age we begin to receive input from others about ourselves. Parents, relatives, and other significant adults provide us with the basis for how we see ourselves. For children with ADD the feedback they receive might be negative ("Sit still!" "Stop fidgeting!" "Why are you so restless?" "Pay attention!"). Over time, these criticisms can be incorporated into one's concept of self. Little by little, children with ADD may come to the realization that they are difficult to be around, a burden to their family and teachers. Fortunately there are many things parents can do to reduce this probability.

First, don't think of self-esteem in general terms, such as "He has low self-esteem, that's why he can't read" (he may have a learning disability) or "She misbehaves because she has low self-esteem" (she may have a significant behavioral disorder). Think of self-esteem as it relates to specific behaviors. For example, your child may have a difficult time staying in his seat in school but is an excellent basketball player. There are many behaviors and skills that are subsumed within each task that children perform that it makes more sense to talk about specific strengths and needs than to use the general term *self-esteem*. The following suggestions can increase children's positive feelings about themselves, their self-esteem:

- Praise them for all their appropriate behaviors.
- Don't criticize them for every minor inappropriate behavior. (See Key 17.)
- Refrain from global labels ("You're lazy," "You're so hyper"). Describe the behavior specifically.
- Find activities that they excel at and provide opportunities for practice.
- Never compare their behavior to that of their siblings.
- Never discuss your child's behavior in their presence (unless it is positive).
- Keep expectations realistic.
- Get help when appropriate, i.e., a tutor for school, counseling for child and/or family.
- Provide activities with success built in.
- Avoid activities where failure is probable.
- Reinforce effort, not just task completion.
- Break tasks into small, manageable components. For example, if you want your child to clean his room, rather than give him a general command to do so break it up as follows:

  Clean Room
  1. All clothes off floor.
  2. All clothes in drawers or closet.
  3. Bed made.
  4. All papers thrown in wastepaper basket.

When you return to the room and still find it in disarray you can simply refer back to each step rather than calling him a "slob" or the room "filthy." You may decide that bed-making needs a lot of assistance so you break that into smaller steps, such as:

Making A Bed
1. Place fitted sheet on mattress.
2. Place flat sheet on bed.
3. Tuck in flat sheet.
4. Place blanket on bed.
5. Tuck in blanket.
6. Put pillow case on pillow.

Once again, if it is not completed satisfactorily you can go back to each step and reinforce what ever was done instead of criticizing what was not done.

Canfield and Wells have a wonderful book entitled *100 Ways to Enhance Self-Concept in the Classroom: A Handbook for Teachers and Parents*. Many of their activities are very useful for parents. Those most appropriate for parents of children with ADD are listed below:

- *Pride Line*. An entire family can do this during mealtime. Each member of the family makes a statement about a specific behavior. They describe something that occurred that day that they are proud of ("I'm proud that..."). Over time, children begin to think of things throughout the day that they can share with their family at dinner time. It helps them focus on the good things that they did throughout the day and start seeing that they are capable of doing many good things.
- *Success a Day*. A variation on the pride line is to have your child write down or tell you one success they

had that day in school ("I tried to do multiplication problems and succeeded" or "I understood most of what I read in science"). Write these in a book. These may overlap with pride statements but the effect is the same, building a reservoir of good feelings about themselves. Periodically review the book and note how many successes they had. We have found that this is particularly good when your child has had a hard time in school that day.

- *Strength Bombardment.* Have your child list all his strengths and you do the same. You can also ask his teacher, coaches, group leaders, any significant adults (grandparents will really increase the size of this list). Try to be as specific as possible and include even small things like "puts dirty clothes in hamper." Start small and you can build. If you only write down major strengths it can be discouraging.

- *Positive Feelings.* Ask your child to respond to the following question: "Can you think of something that a grownup did or said to you this week that made you feel good?" If your child cannot think of anything, you need to go back to the beginning of this Key and implement some of the suggestions. But most likely your child will have something to say and that can be a clue to you as to what is important to your child and what makes her feel good.

- *Twenty Things I Like To Do.* Ask your child to dictate or list these things and you can use it as a list of potential reinforcers. You may probably know most of the twenty items listed, but you may find a few surprises, which makes this activity worthwhile.

- *Words That Describe Me.* Ask your child to give you three words to describe herself. Then have her list what specific behaviors a person with those traits exhibits. For example, if your child says "I'm nice," ask her what do nice people do? Then list what she says (you can help out). This will enable her to see the specific behaviors that are connected to such descriptors and will help her view herself in a more precise manner, as opposed to a broad label. If your child writes down negative statements, have her rewrite the "bad" words so they describe exactly what she did. Such as "I'm dumb in math" to "I haven't learned the multiplication tables." Those rewritten statements do not imply worthlessness or helplessness, but rather show that something can be done to change the condition.

The overall goal of all of the above is to provide children with experiences that will make them feel good about themselves. Obviously, this is important for everyone, but it is especially important for those children who, through no fault of their own, find it difficult to comply with so many societal rules of appropriate behavior.

24

$\blacktriangle\blacktriangle\blacktriangle\blacktriangle\blacktriangle\blacktriangle\blacktriangle\blacktriangle\blacktriangle$

TEACHING CHILDREN TO MONITOR THEIR BEHAVIOR

A s children with ADD grow older, they should be able to monitor some of their behaviors themselves. This is especially true as they enter high school. This Key will present some strategies that parents can employ in order to assist their children in this process.

If you are carrying out a behavioral program at home that requires the use of points or stars on a chart, you can encourage your child to become more involved in the counting and the placement of stars on the chart. Over time, you can have him record some of his behavior throughout the day ("Count how many minutes it took you to get dressed" or "Count the number of days you remembered to bring your assignment pad home"). We know of youngsters with ADD who count and chart the number of times they "get mad" at their parents. We know of children who chart the amount of time their thumb is in their mouths or the times they look out the window in school or daydream. For many children awareness of when they are engaged in a behavior may help reduce some of these behaviors. This is not always easy in that some students may find it reinforcing to get so much attention that they continue to engage in the inappropriate behavior. Remember that the reinforcement for self-recording and reduction of the behavior must be powerful.

97

Self-recording is very helpful for getting ready for school or hygiene. A child we work with has an erasable chart on his bathroom wall that lists the following:

1. Take shower.
2. Dry hair.
3. Comb hair.
4. Brush teeth.
5. Use toilet.

Every night he checks off each task and receives a reward at the end of the week for a specified number of checks. He takes pride in his ability to "take care of myself."

Self-instruction is another technique that many children with ADD can successfully use. Instead of parents providing prompts for the child, they do so themselves. Most adults do this, as do many children. Before you attempt a difficult task you may say things like "Remember, take one step at a time, check each part..." or when playing a sport you go over each step to aid you in acquiring the skill. Self-instruction has been successful in reducing inattention behaviors in children described as hyperactive and impulsive. The general sequence parents should follow is:

1. You perform the task while talking aloud. "I'm getting my toothbrush, picking up the toothpaste, placing it on the brush..."
2. Have your child copy your behavior *as you provide instruction.* ("Go to the sink, take your toothbrush ...")
3. Have your child engage in the task and talk aloud.
4. Have your child engage in the task and whisper.
5. Finally, have your child perform the task and "talk to himself."

It is helpful if this technique can also be done in the classroom. Many teachers (usually special educators) routinely employ such procedures while children are taught to use "self-talk" to monitor their own behavior.

Some children with ADD may need to seek the help of a professional to assist them in self-monitoring. And for other children it may not be appropriate. Self-monitoring seems to be most effective for children who have mild to moderate ADD and for adolescents. Peer pressure is great incentive for adolescents to reduce their hyperactive, impulsive, and distractible behaviors. The behaviors that were tolerated by peers at an early age are no longer acceptable to teenagers. By teaching adolescents to monitor their own behavior you are allowing them to have greater control over themselves. There are teenagers who self-record their own homework compliance and appropriate eating behavior and who employ self-instruction to get themselves to class on time and reduce anxiety during tests. Some students find it useful to wear wrist golf counters to record behavior. They look like a watch and are inconspicuous. The child or adolescent wears the wrist golf counter and records each behavior. The counters can be used for calling out in class, thumb sucking, nail biting, pencil tapping, temper tantrums, and vulgar language, to name a few behaviors. Knowledge of results appears to be a powerful reinforcer for adolescents and to a lesser extent with children. If your child is younger than twelve, you will probably need to employ some external reinforcements in addition to knowledge of results.

Self-monitoring is one tool in a behavioral repertoire, certainly not the only one and not appropriate for all children with ADD. In those cases where it is appropriate, it can be powerful because it allows the child to have some self-control. It can show him them that he is capable of changing his own behavior. The ability to monitor his own behavior will enable him to be more positive when he approaches other problems because he has a strategy. Also, it's beneficial for parents in that you have one less behavior to deal with.

There are other interventions that encourage self-monitoring. One of these is counseling. Many children and adolescents with ADD benefit from counseling. In counseling they can learn about their own difficulties and successful ways to deal with them. It is critical that parents as well as children attend these sessions because ADD has an impact on all members of the family. Whenever possible, *all* members of the family should attend the counseling sessions. These group meetings must be at the discretion of the professional, but they should occur at some designated time. In counseling, the child not only will come to a better understanding of the disorder but will develop effective strategies for coping with ADD.

25

~~~~~~

DEALING WITH SIBLINGS

A child with ADD, regardless of the severity, will have an impact on all family members, not just parents. The purpose of this Key is to address some of the issues related to siblings and to provide parents with resources for their children who do not have ADD.

Much has been written about siblings of a disabled child. The responses to the disability vary tremendously, depending upon a number of variables, such as age, sex, and severity of the disability. However, some general issues involving resentment, embarrassment, and guilt present themselves.

Children may resent the time parents must spend with their sibling with ADD. They also may feel that the money spent for medical expenses, counseling, or special camps could be put to some other use in the family. Some siblings have told us of the different set of rules for their siblings with ADD. All of this can lead to resentment and anger if not handled appropriately.

As siblings get older, one common theme is embarrassment. How do they explain their brother's or sister's behavior to their friends? When they are on a family outing are people staring at them? Adolescence is an age where almost anything parents or other family members do can bring about a feeling of embarrassment. Therefore, it should not be surprising that acting out or impulsive behavior may cause sisters and brothers concern.

Not surprisingly, many siblings have discussed the guilt involved in having such feelings. But guilt is not the only feeling. The wide range of feelings experienced by siblings is complex and defies easy categorization. What is clear is that they must be dealt with in a nonthreatening manner. Many siblings can benefit from short-term counseling or family counseling to deal with these issues.

You shouldn't be discouraged because the picture is not so gloomy. There are numerous accounts of very positive interactions and relationships among siblings. Many families report extraordinary examples of caring, warmth, and compassion, as well as a willingness to help out when needed on the part of their children who do not have ADD. And research on siblings of children with various disabilities, from mild to severe, indicates that the impact on their lives has many positive aspects.

Where does this leave you? Siblings of children with any disability or disorder will be affected. They will experience a wide range of emotions that may change throughout their lifetime. Some will be positive, some will be negative. What is most important, however, is how parents deal with this situation. In addition to individual counseling and/or family counseling, there are sibling support groups throughout the country (see Appendix C; Resources for Siblings). These are not geared specifically to ADD, but you may find one that is appropriate. Because ADD is a "popular" topic you may begin to notice a number of books written expressly for children. A word of caution. Read the books yourself first to see if the message is one you are comfortable with. There may be specific interventions employed with the characters in the book that are not appropriate for all children with ADD and you need to decide on the appropriateness before giving it to any of your children. Also, you may find some of the descriptions of behaviors associated with ADD to be inconsistent with that of your child. Select books with care.

What follows are some general guidelines for dealing with siblings:

Accept Their Feelings

Don't deny the fact that your child with ADD will have some impact on siblings. At times this may be manifested in an angry outburst or an insensitive remark toward you or your child with ADD. And while such behavior shouldn't be condoned, you can find an appropriate time to discuss the feelings that lead to such an outburst. Simple statements, such as, "I know it seems like we spend a lot of money on Todd" or "I'm sorry, but right now he needs a little more of our time," can help convey your feeling that you know it's not always easy dealing with a difference in the family. You might want to try the following activity suggested by the National Association of Sibling Programs:

Make a time capsule. "Times" are listed on pieces of paper and placed in a time capsule (anything can be used such as plastic eggs, a treasure chest, etc). Then a capsule is selected and the "time" noted inside is discussed.

Suggested "times" to place in capsule:

- A time when I really felt proud of my brother or sister.
- A time when I really was embarrassed by my brother or sister.
- A time when my brother or sister caused problems with a friend.

- A time I helped my brother or sister in a special way.
- A time my brother or sister helped me in a special way.
- A time my brother or sister really made me mad.
- A time my brother or sister made me laugh.

Don't Try to Make Them Feel Guilty for not Having ADD

We have overheard parents remark, "You should be thankful that you're not —." Most kids probably don't think in terms of having or not having difficulties. They are who they are. To suggest that they behave in a certain way because they don't have a specific disorder or disability is unfair and will not change their behavior. We know of youngsters who screamed back at their parents, "I wish I did have—because then you'd treat me better." All of this provocative language cannot lead to a resolution of the problem. It's better to avoid such guilt-ridden and confrontational statements.

Try to Spend Special Time with Siblings

There's no getting away from the fact that parenting a child with ADD takes a great deal of time. Given the pressures of everyday life, it is hard to find time for scheduling more activities. You should try, however, to come up with some special time for siblings. It can be a drive to the store or watching a TV show together, just some time alone with parents.

Appendix C lists a number of resources that parents might find useful.

26

~~~~~~

MONITORING TREATMENT

The treatment of ADD requires a comprehensive intervention program, including professionals from the fields of psychology and education, and, when appropriate, from medicine. Keeping track of such intervention is not an easy job, but one that is important for the success of the program. One of the major problems encountered by parents of children with ADD is the lack of communication among professionals. Therefore, parents frequently have an undue burden of fostering communication among all the professionals who work with their child. This Key provides some suggestions for communicating in a reasonable, time-efficient manner.

From Diagnosis to Treatment

Diagnosis of ADD must be based upon findings from a number of professionals. The evaluation process should include medical, psychological, and educational evaluations as well as a thorough social history. Based on these findings, a treatment plan will be implemented. Without such a multidisciplinary approach, parents run the risk of misdiagnosis or poorly controlled intervention plans. It is critical that everyone working with the child is kept abreast of the treatment and has input into its effectiveness.

Monitoring Medication

Children on medication for ADD should be carefully monitored. One of the major criticisms of the use of medication is the lack of communication between the physician and school personnel. We know of too many cases where the only communication is the parent asking the teacher, "How is he doing?" and the teacher responding, "Much better." In order for the effectiveness of the medication to be evaluated, there should be ongoing communication between the school and the physician and between the parent and the school. One simple way to start such an evaluation process is by employing the Medication Effects Rating Scale, developed by Harvey L. Parker, Ph.D.

The teacher fills out a simple checklist and gives it to the parent and physician. This assists the physician in evaluating the effectiveness of the medication. If there are no observable changes in the child's behavior, perhaps the use of medication, the dosage, or the method of delivery needs to be re-evaluated. If, while medicated, the child's behavior in school does not improve, then perhaps the treatment should be discontinued.

If your child is receiving special education services, it is likely that the teacher will be skilled in the principles and techniques of applied behavior analysis. If this is the case, the teachers will be able to carry out a more thorough evaluation of the behavior in the classroom using these procedures. Talk to your child's teacher and ask him to contact the physician. This will allow you to make sound decisions regarding the effectiveness of medication. Medicating children and adolescents with ADD is a sensitive topic for parents, making it extremely important to monitor the results. Although the physician should seek input from the school, the crucial link is the parents. Parents who are persistent in their requests for such communication usually receive it.

Monitoring Counseling and Behavioral Interventions

The treatment of ADD will require some type of behavioral approach and/or counseling for the child and/or family. How do you know if these are working? How can you be sure that they are bringing about the desired changes? The multidisciplinary approach to diagnosis and treatment requires a program coordinator. After the initial treatment plan has been developed, specific behavioral tasks should be identified, for example, redirect fidgeting, increase on-task behavior in school, reduce temper outbursts at home. Throughout the treatment, these behaviors should be evaluated by each professional. Moreover, some mechanism should exist where all professionals can share the results. Dr. Paul Wender, a psychiatrist at the University of Utah Medical School, who has written widely on the subject of ADD, suggests that the psychiatrist be the coordinator of the treatment program, obtaining information about the child from various sources and prescribing treatments such as medication, behavioral therapy, family counseling, and special education services. This type of coordination is extremely helpful, if not crucial. That is why a medical center that has services geared specifically for ADD is so useful. The program plan will be closely monitored by a professional who will keep abreast of the child's performance in school and home and who will have avenues for information from psychologists, social workers, teachers, and other professionals.

If such a medical center is not available to you, does it mean you are doomed to failure? Not at all. It simply means that you will have to assume the role of coordinator. For example, a behavioral program to reduce behaviors at home won't necessarily reduce them in school unless these professionals talk to each other about generalizing the interven-

107

tion. This is why it is critical that the parent function as coordinator. Keeping good records of treatment and recommendations made by professionals, fostering communication among professionals, and frequently following up on contacts among professionals will allow you to monitor the treatment plan. Also, if you and your child are receiving counseling it is a good idea if the teacher speaks to the person doing the counseling in order to better understand how to deal with your child in school. Only nonconfidential information is shared, with the goal being to deliver a comprehensive program that will meet the needs of your child. We have had numerous experiences where behavioral or other therapeutic interventions were employed without communication among the various professionals and the home. The teacher was unaware of what was going on and therefore could not provide the best services for the child. Without knowledge of the program, the teacher employed techniques that were contrary to those used by mental health professionals.

The major responsibility for monitoring treatment will probably fall on your shoulders. Don't be intimidated about asking questions ("How will I know this is working?" or "Shouldn't I be seeing a change in her behavior?"). As a consumer of services, you are entitled to answers. More important, professionals with expertise in this area will want coordination among all professionals and the home. If they don't, perhaps they are not the best practitioners for your child. (In Appendix A; Resources for Parents, you will find groups that can assist you when selecting professionals to help you with your child. These parents have had similar problems and are more than willing to help you.)

Part Four

WORKING WITH
YOUR SCHOOL

Parents of children and adolescents with ADD must develop a close working relationship with school personnel for a number of reasons. First, you need to monitor the effectiveness of the treatment. For example, if your child is receiving medication it is crucial that you are in close communication with the teacher in order to see if the medication is working. Second, you need to be a strong advocate for your child. Establishing a good relationship with school staff will enable you to have some impact on your child's program. And most important, you need to develop consistency between home and school. When the parents and teachers communicate in a cooperative fashion, the child will reap the benefits.

27

^^

KNOW YOUR RIGHTS

Federal legislation mandating special education services is relatively new. As of 1975, with the passage of the Education of the Handicapped Act (also referred to as Public Law 94-142), all children with special educational needs must be provided with a free, appropriate public education. Before 1975, the quantity and quality of services provided was dictated by where you lived; some states had programs, others didn't. Some parents of children with special needs would move to a different state or a different community in order for their child to receive the needed educational services. During the congressional hearings that led to the passage of P.L. 94-142, it was found that half of all the children with special educational needs were not being provided with any services whatsoever. For parents of children with ADD this was a major concern until recently when the Individuals with Disabilities Act (IDEA), also referred to as Public Law 101-476, included a memorandum that specified that children with ADD be eligible for special education services (see Key 36). The 1997 amendments to IDEA reinforced and strengthened this provision.

Our national consciousness was raised with the passage of federal legislation that assured parents that their disabled child would receive educational services from age three until age eighteen. However, the school district was not mandated to provide services to the three to five age group unless they had a school program for nondisabled three- to five-year-olds. In 1986, P.L. 99-457 extended these services to all disabled children in the three to five age group.

Parents now have specific regulations that are implemented by the federal, state, and local governments that ensure that the services to which they and their disabled children are entitled are forthcoming.

A Right to an Education

Most parents take for granted that they can bring their five-year-old to kindergarten registration and their child will be enrolled. Before P.L. 94-142, however, parents of children with special needs were not provided with this basic right. They paid the same school taxes as their neighbors and their portion of federal and state taxes used for education was the same, but they could not count on their children receiving an education.

Many schools felt they were unable to provide an education for special education students; they didn't have the personnel, the facilities, or the equipment. But, moreover, it was an issue concerning the value of an education and what constitutes an education. Should a severely retarded child receive an education? Should a deaf-blind child receive an education? Should an autistic child receive an education? These and similar types of questions were debated for years before any legislation, and there were and still are differences of opinion.

Also questioned was what is an education? Should it be defined as the acquisition of academic skills? If so, what about those who would never acquire those skills? The hearings surrounding the passage of the Education of the Handicapped Act provided a focus for experts, parents, and legislation on all sides of the issue. The conclusion was that if any child in a school district is entitled to an education, then *all* children are entitled. The needs of each child must be considered. Children must receive an education, and it is the responsibility of the local school district to develop an appropriate educational plan. The recognition that *all* children must be provided with an education set the stage for provisions regarding the quality of such an education.

A Right to a Free, Appropriate Education

The education for special education students must be appropriate to their needs and provided at no cost to the parents. If the most appropriate placement is a special school with a wide variety of support services, such as speech therapy, physical therapy, and psychological services, then the student must receive these services. The spirit of the law is clear: all children are entitled to an education and this right should not be dictated by the parents' ability to pay.

In order to ensure that each special education student is provided with an appropriate education, the authors of P.L. 94-142 required the inclusion of an Individualized Education Program, commonly referred to as an I.E.P. The format of the I.E.P. differs from school district to school district, but must always include the following:

1. The student's current level of performance in the areas of concern.
2. Annual and short-term objectives.
3. The specific education services to be provided and the extent to which the student will participate in regular education.
4. The projected date for initiation of the program and anticipated duration of such services.
5. A description of the schedules and evaluation procedures for determining whether objectives are being met.

Parent participation is necessary if the I.E.P. is to be a useful document. Schools must involve parents in each step of the process.

An important component of the I.E.P. is the Least Restrictive Environment statement. The school must state to what extent your child is being educated in the *mainstream,* that is, regular classroom instruction. The law is very clear; it states that "the handicapped child should be educated with his nonhandicapped peer to the maximum extent possible." Special education students do not need to be isolated in order to achieve. Conversely, some students' needs are best met in a more restrictive setting, such as a special school. The point of the Least Restrictive Environment statement is that all children have the right to learn in an environment consistent with their academic, social, and physical needs. By providing for individual needs, the letter and the spirit of the law is observed.

A Right to a Nondiscriminatory Evaluation

In the recent past, students who could not speak English were evaluated in English and placed into special education based on that evaluation. This can no longer take place; students must be evaluated in their native language. Therefore, if the child is Spanish-speaking, the evaluation must be in Spanish and all written information must be translated at all school meetings that parents attend. If a student's processing mode of communication is sign language, then the same holds true. An interpreter must be present to sign the entire evaluation, and if the parents need an interpreter, the school must provide one at no cost to the parents. All of this has been established to ensure that students are referred, identified, and placed in special education settings based on a nondiscriminatory process.

113

Parents must be advocates for their children and be willing to request appropriate services. A child cannot be evaluated without parental permission and if a parent feels that an evaluation solely in English would be unfair to the child, she should request an evaluation in the child's primary language. A simple translation of the test is not sufficient. Rather the evaluators must be aware of the linguistic and cultural needs of the student, and it is up to the school district to ensure that these types of services are provided. There is considerable evidence in the professional literature to suggest that many students are placed in special education settings based on examiner and testing bias. Parents must be aware of their rights in this matter if they are to ensure an appropriate, nondiscriminatory education for their child.

A Right to Due Process

Perhaps the most important of all rights is the right to due process under the law. Parents are to be kept fully informed at every stage if they are in disagreement with any decision. Specifically parents have the right to:

- Review all school records.
- Review assessment procedures (underlying test).
- Refuse or permit evaluation.
- Be informed of the results of the evaluation.
- Be provided with an independent "second opinion" at public expense.
- Participate in multidisciplinary team meetings.

If you disagree with the findings of the school district, you are entitled to a *due process hearing*, also referred to as an *impartial hearing*. The specific manner in which you request such a hearing varies from state to state. Check with your local Director of Special Education or Director of Pupil

Personnel Services. In general, the law stipulates the following:

- You must be informed of free or low-cost legal or other relevant services.
- An unbiased, impartial hearing officer (he or she cannot be employed by the school district) will give you and other advocates for your child an opportunity to present your side of the issue.
- You are entitled to a written or topic-recorded, word-for-word record of the proceedings.
- You are entitled to interpreters of the deaf and/or interpreter of the language spoken in your home at no expense.
- You are entitled to be represented by an attorney and/or other professionals and any other persons of your choice can accompany you to the hearing.
- You and your attorney can cross-examine officials from the school district.
- All information presented must be shared with you at least five school days before the hearing.

You will be informed of the hearing within forty-five calendar days of your request. You may appeal your decision to the Commissioner of Education in your state. Unless you choose otherwise, your child remains in his current placement until all proceedings are completed.

The reason for these provisions is not to establish an adversarial relationship between parents and schools. Rather, it is to ensure a free, appropriate, public education for all children. The right to due process helps to keep this vision intact.

28

A PRIMER ON IDEA 1997

The Council for Exceptional Children in their publication CEC Today (April/May, 1999) provided highlights for IDEA 1997. Those related to ADHD are:

Other Health Impairment

Attention deficit disorder and attention deficit hyperactivity disorder may result in eligibility for special education services under the "other health impairment" category. This is the first time ADHD is specifically noted in IDEA.

Supplementary Aids and Supports

Supplementary aids and services includes aids, services, and other supports that are provided in general education settings to enable children with disabilities to be educated with nondisabled children to the maximum extent appropriate. This can include a computer, one to one aid, and/or an auditory trainer (FM Unit), to name a few.

Service plans

Services and Aids That Benefit Children with Disabilities

A school may use funds for special education, related services, and supplementary aids and services provided in a general education setting for a child with a disability, even if children without disabilities receive incidental benefit from the services. This is very important because it relates to specific strategies for students with ADHD.

Mediation

School and state education agencies must ensure that procedures are established and implemented to allow parents and schools to resolve their differences through mediation.

Evaluation

When evaluating a student for eligibility for special education, schools must

- Assess the child in all areas of suspected disability, including cognitive, behavioral, physical, and developmental factors.
- Use a variety of assessment tools and strategies to gather functional and developmental information. The assessment tools and strategies must also help determine the child's educational needs.
- Include information from the parent that can help determine whether the child has a disability and the content of the I.E.P.
- Gather information related to the child's involvement and progress in the general education curriculum.
- Obtain informed consent from the parent before the evaluation is conducted. The agency may continue to pursue an evaluation if the parents refuse consent by using mediation and due process procedures.

IEPs

IDEA 1997 added new I.E.P. requirements and expanded existing requirements. The I.E.P. must include

- A statement of the child's present levels of educational performance including how the child's disability affects his or her involvement and progress in the general education curriculum. For preschool children, it must describe how the disability affects the child's participation in appropriate activities.
- A statement of measurable annual goals, including benchmarks or short-term objectives related to

(A) Meeting the child's needs that result from his or her disability and enable the child to be involved in and progress in the general education curriculum.

(B) Meeting each of the child's other educational needs that result from the child's disability.

- A statement of the special education, related services, and supplementary aids to be provided to the child, or on behalf of the child. Such statement should also include any program modifications or supports for school personnel that are needed for the child to be involved in and progress in the general education curriculum; to participate in extracurricular and other nonacademic activities; and to be educated and participate with children with and without disabilities.

- The extent to which the child will not participate with children without disabilities in the general education class.

- Any modification in the administration of statewide or districtwide assessments that are needed for the child to participate in the assessment.

- If the child will not participate in the assessment or part of the assessment, a statement explaining why that assessment is not appropriate and how the child will be assessed.

- The projected date for the beginning of the services and modifications and their frequency, location, and duration.

- The child's transition service needs (beginning at the age 14 and updated annually) that focus on his or her courses of study. This should include, when appropriate, the interagency responsibilities or needed linkages (beginning at age 16 or younger) and a statement that the child has been informed of the rights that will transfer to him or her on reaching the age of majority under state law.

- How the child's progress toward the annual goals will be measured and the extent to which the child's progress will enable him or her to achieve the goals by the end of the year.

- How the child's parents will be regularly informed of their child's progress at least as often as parents of nondisabled children are informed.

Including Parents in the I.E.P. Team

Each LEA or state education agency (SEA) must ensure that the parents of each child with a disability are members of any group that makes decisions on the educational placement of their child.

Including General Education Teachers in the I.E.P. Team

- If the child participates or may be participating in the general education environment, the I.E.P. team must include at least one of the student's general education teachers. The teacher must participate in the development, review, and revision of the child's I.E.P. The general education teacher must also help determine appropriate positive behavioral interventions and strategies for the child, as well as any supplementary aids, and program modifications and supports for school personnel that will be provided on the child's behalf.

Access to the I.E.P.

The I.E.P. of a child with a disability must be accessible to each general education teacher—as well as to each special education teacher, related service provider, and other service providers—who is responsible for implementing the I.E.P.

- Each teacher must be informed of his or her specific responsibilities related to implementing the I.E.P. and the accommodations and supports the child will receive. This is of critical importance for students with ADHD.

Discipline

Behavioral Assessments and Behavioral Interventions

- I.E.P. team meetings to develop a behavioral assessment plan or review a current behavioral intervention plan are required only when the child has been removed from his or her placement for more than ten school days in a school year and/or when removing the child constitutes a change in placement.
- After removing the child for more than ten consecutive days or beginning action to remove a child and change his or her placement, the I.E.P. team must meet within ten school days to plan a functional behavioral assessment and implement a behavioral plan to address the problem behavior. If the child already has a behavior intervention plan, the I.E.P. team should review the plan and modify it to address the behavior.
- If subsequent removals occur, the I.E.P. team members review the child's behavioral intervention plan and its implementation to determine if it should be modified. The I.E.P. team meets only if one or more team members believe that modifications are necessary.

Parent Appeal and Child Placement

- Parents who disagree with any decision regarding placement may request a hearing. If they do, the SEA or LEA must arrange for an expedited hearing. During the appeal, the child remains in the IAES pending the hearing officer's decision or until the 45-day time limit ends, whichever occurs first.
- If a child is placed in an IAES and the school proposes to change the child's placement after the IAES ends, the child remains in his or her current placement (the placement before the IAES). However, if a hearing officer determines that there is a likelihood of injury to the child or others in his or her prior placement, the placement may be changed.

29

INCLUSION

Inclusion—educating all children in regular classes regardless of disability—is a topic of heated discussion in special education circles, but for students with ADD it does not represent a major change in the way they have been receiving special education services. The advocacy board of the Center on Human Policy at Syracuse University has the following statement on inclusion:

Inclusion Means:

1. Educating all children with disabilities in regular classrooms regardless of the nature of their disabling condition(s).
2. Providing all students with enhanced opportunities to learn from each other's contributions.
3. Providing necessary services within the regular schools.
4. Supporting regular teachers and administrators (e.g., by providing time, training, teamwork, resources, and strategies).
5. Having students with disabilities follow the same schedules as nondisabled students.
6. Involving students with disabilities in age-appropriate academic classes and extracurricular activities, including art, music, gym, field trips, assemblies, and graduation exercises.
7. Allowing students with disabilities to use the school cafeteria, library, playground, and other facilities along with nondisabled students.

8. Encouraging friendships between nondisabled and disabled students.
9. Allowing students with disabilities to receive their education and job training in regular community environments when appropriate.
10. Teaching all children to understand and accept human differences.
11. Placing children with disabilities in the same schools they would attend if they did not have disabilities.
12. Taking parents' concerns seriously.
13. Providing an appropriate individualized educational program.

Inclusion Does Not Mean:

1. Dumping students with disabilities into regular programs without preparation or support.
2. Providing special services in separate or isolated places.
3. Ignoring children's individual needs.
4. Jeopardizing students' safety or well-being.
5. Placing unreasonable demands on teachers or administrators.
6. Ignoring parents' concerns.
7. Isolating students with disabilities in regular schools.
8. Placing students with disabilities in schools or classes that are not age appropriate.
9. Requiring that students be "ready" and earn their way into regular classrooms based on cognitive or social skills.

Much more research needs to be undertaken before inclusionary placements can be deemed more effective than other special education settings. This issue will continue to be a topic of debate among special education professionals and parents alike.

In January 1993 the Learning Disabilities Association of America issued a Position Paper on inclusion. It is presented here below.

The Learning Disabilities Association of America, LDA, is a national not-for-profit organization of parents, professionals, and persons with learning disabilities concerned about the welfare of individuals with learning disabilities. During the 1990–1991 school year, 2,117,087 children in public schools in the United States were identified as having learning disabilities. This is more than 50 percent of the total number of students identified in all disability categories, included many students diagnosed with ADD.

"Full inclusion," "full integration," "unified system," "inclusive education" are terms used to describe a popular policy/practice in which all students with disabilities, regardless of the nature or the severity of the disability and need for related services, receive their total education in their home school.

The Learning Disabilities Association of America does not support "full inclusion" or any policies that mandate the same placement, instruction, or treatment for **ALL** students with learning disabilities. Many students with learning disabilities benefit from being served in the regular education classroom. However, the regular education classroom is not the appropriate placement for a number of students with learning disabilities who may need alternative instructional environments, teaching strategies, and/or materials that cannot or will not be provided within the context of a regular classroom placement.

LDA believes that decisions regarding educational placement of students with disabilities must be based on the needs of each individual student rather than administrative convenience or budgetary considerations and must be the result of a cooperative effort involving the educators, parents, and the student when appropriate.

LDA strongly supports the Individuals with Disabilities Education Act (IDEA) which mandates:

- A free and appropriate public education in the least restrictive environment appropriate for the students' specific learning needs.
- A team approved Individualized Education Program (I.E.P.) that includes current functioning levels, instructional goals and objectives, placement and services decisions, and procedures for evaluation of program effectiveness.
- A placement decision must be made on an individual basis and considered only after the development of the I.E.P.
- A continuum of alternative placements to meet the needs of students with disabilities for special education and related services.
- A system for the continuing education of regular and special education and related services personnel to enable these personnel to meet the needs of children with disabilities.

LDA believes that the placement of **ALL** children with disabilities in the regular education classroom is a great violation of IDEA as is the placement of **ALL** children in separate classrooms on the basis of their type of disability.

LDA urges the U.S. Department of Education and each state to move deliberately and reflectively in school restructuring, using the Individuals with Disabilities Education Act as a foundation—mindful of the best interest of all children with disabilities.

30

SUPPORT SERVICES

The school psychologist, school social worker, guidance counselor, reading teacher, speech and language pathologist, and other specialists provide support services to children with ADD. The focus of this Key is on a group of people who play an important function in our schools. Depending upon the terminology used by your own school, they may be referred to as *support services, ancillary services, child study teams, prereferral teams,* or *building level teams*. They represent a wide variety of services that are provided to students as they progress through the school years.

Following is a brief description of the roles of various professionals who provide much needed services in our schools. Although licensing varies from state to state, most of these positions require either a master's or a doctorate degree, and considerable supervision before working in a school setting. To be sure, there will be overlap between the roles of the various professionals, and individuals occupying these positions may take on different and/or additional responsibilities. If you ever feel unsure about the boundaries of expertise, consult with your child's principal.

School Psychologist

The major responsibility of most school psychologists is to assess the intellectual and social-emotional status of students. School psychologists are frequently called upon to administer individual intelligence tests when there is a question of a student's ability to perform in school, and to evaluate a student's social-emotional status when this becomes a concern of parents and school personnel.

In addition to these responsibilities, school psychologists meet with individual or groups of students to discuss issues that concern them, consult with teachers to determine the most effective way to deal with specific students, and talk to parents about their child's school-related behavior. If a student is encountering a problem that is beyond the scope of the school, the school psychologist can make appropriate referrals to the parent.

School Social Workers

Depending upon the school district, the grade level, or the principal, the responsibilities of the school social worker may include providing services to students and staff, such as direction and referrals to outside mental health facilities and public welfare agencies; providing information on substance abuse, alcoholism, and child abuse; and meeting with parent groups. School social workers may also provide counseling services on an individual or group basis dealing with a wide variety of issues that may include separation, divorce, depression, peer pressure, or suicide, thus enabling students to deal with these difficult concerns through emotional support and reassurance. When the needs of the student and family cannot be accommodated in a school setting, the social worker can give parents the name and number of an appropriate individual or agency.

Guidance Counselor

The majority of guidance counselors are employed on the secondary level (middle/junior/high school). Typically, they are responsible for assisting students with the selection of classes, career counseling, and postsecondary placements (college/vocational/employment). However, they may engage in other activities. They may work with groups of students who are not working up to their potential; they may smooth the transition from middle/junior high school to high school; and they may encourage teacher-student communication, especially when students are mainstreamed into regular classes. They are also able to make appropriate referrals when the problem is beyond their expertise.

Reading Specialist

Most students learn to read with little or no difficulty. However, a small group of students encounter considerable trouble with this task. For them, the services provided by the reading specialist can be invaluable.

Students are usually referred to this specialist by their classroom teacher when it is apparent that reading skills are not progressing at an appropriate rate. The reading specialist will then administer individual or small group diagnostic reading tests that will enable her to determine the current level of performance, the student's strengths and weaknesses, and information that will be useful in selecting the best reading approach. If the problem appears to be more than just reading, an appropriate referral can be made.

Most instruction is provided in small group or individual sessions and in consultation with the regular classroom teacher. Reading specialists will also work directly with regular classroom teachers in order to improve reading instruction on a school-wide basis.

Speech and Language Pathologist

When a child's speech or language does not meet chronological age expectations, he is often referred to a speech and language pathologist. A thorough assessment of speech and language functions would be undertaken and an appropriate intervention plan developed.

Problems in articulation, voice disorders, and stuttering represents only a small part of the speech or language pathologist's responsibility. They spend considerable time working with students who have difficulty understanding language and being able to express their thoughts through language, both oral and written. They also refer students to appropriate personnel if the problems encountered by students are greater than a speech or language impairment.

Parents who know the roles and responsibilities of the support personnel will be better able to advocate for their children.

31

^^^

UNDERSTANDING STANDARDIZED TEST SCORES

N
o doubt sometime in your child's school career you will be confronted with results of standardized tests. Throughout the course of the evaluation for the identification of ADD and through the school year, these results may be used to determine school readiness, class placement, and course selection. By understanding the test results you will be better equipped to make informed decisions.

Types of Tests

Most standardized tests can be categorized as intellectual and aptitude, achievement, or diagnostic tests. It is important to know the type of test administered to children because each yields unique kinds of results.

Intellectual (Intelligence) Tests

These tests are employed by most school districts to screen for intellectual impairment and to assess student potential. Sometime during the intermediate grades (fourth, fifth, and sixth) and then again sometime during the high school years, students are given paper and pencil intelligence tests such as the Otis-Lennon. These tests yield an intelligence quotient, frequently referred to as an *I.Q.* score or simply *I.Q.*

Intelligence tests have been challenged in the court because of their inability to predict school performance and their bias against certain racial or ethnic groups; therefore, many of them have been renamed. What were once called intelligence tests are frequently referred to as *learning ability, cognitive batteries,* or simply *ability tests.*

An I.Q. score that falls between 90 and 110 is considered average. Depending upon how far in either direction the score is from this average range, further testing may be indicated.

If the student appears to be significantly above or below average on a group administered test, an individual intelligence test, such as the Wechsler Intelligence Scale for Children-Revised (WISC-R) and the Stanford-Binet Test of Intelligence, may be used in order to better estimate the child's abilities. There are differences between the group-administered and individually-administered tests. The former takes little time and can be given by a person with minimal training, whereas the latter is usually administered by a licensed school psychologist.

Aptitude Tests

Aptitude tests attempt to measure traits and abilities necessary for future success in a given field. Usually students are given aptitude tests, such as the Differential Aptitude Test, toward the end of middle or junior high school in order to determine a course of study or area of interest or ability. As is the case with all tests, these results are never to be used by themselves alone.

Achievement Tests

These tests are usually administered by the classroom teacher at least once per year. Achievement tests are the most frequently used and probably the most recognizable tests employed by schools. The more popular achievement tests are the C.A.T. (California Achievement Tests), the S.A.T. (Stanford Achievement Tests), or the Iowa Basics (The Iowa Test of Basic Skills).

These and other similar tests measure how a student compares in achievement of skills to a large standardized sample of his grade in a particular curricular area, such as reading. Recently, a large number of states have developed their own achievement tests to measure how well a particular group of students performs a skill, such as writing, reading, or math at specific grade levels.

As is the case with intelligence tests, if a student appears to be significantly above or below grade level, an individually-administered achievement test can be used to measure academic skill achievement.

Diagnostic Tests

Diagnostic tests are not routinely administered in school. These tests are reserved for students who are suspected of having a learning or behavioral problem. The most useful type of standardized test, diagnostic tests yield information that is educationally relevant about learner performance. This information enables a teacher to develop a systematic intervention plan.

How to Interpret Tests

Two important characteristics of all standardized tests are validity and reliability. *Validity* refers to how well a test measures what it is supposed to measure. *Reliability* refers to the consistency and stability of the test results when the test is administered on different occasions.

Both validity and reliability are arrived at through statistical analysis, and these numbers are readily available from children's teachers. If parents are concerned about a particular test, they may want to meet with the person who is responsible for their school district's testing and discuss whether the tests used in the school are valid and reliable measures.

Understanding Test Scores

Standardized test scores are obtained by comparing a student's performance with the performance of other students who have taken the test. Derived scores are then reported in a number of ways, the most frequent being grade equivalent, age equivalent, percentile ranks, and stanines.

Grade Equivalent (G.E.)

G.E. is expressed in two numbers separated by a decimal point. The school year (September through June) is divided into tenths, and each month is represented as one tenth. For example, a grade equivalent of 4.5 is interpreted as January of the fourth grade; a 9.1 is September of the ninth grade, and 3.7 is March of the third grade.

The student's performance should be presented as a range of scores rather than as an exact number. If a student received a grade equivalent of 4.5 and the Standard Error of Measurement is 0.3, then the range is 4.2 to 4.8. This is a much more accurate description of a student's performance than a single score. However, even when presented with this range, also called *bands of confidence* grade equivalents, must only be used in the most general way to indicate performance that is somewhat below average or somewhat above average. For example, if a fourth grade student received a G.E. of 12.5 in reading, does it mean he should be moved to a twelfth grade group? No, it merely means that he performed the way a twelfth grader would have if he took the same tests.

Age Equivalent (A.E.)

A.E. scores are also based on the average student's performance on a particular test, but instead of using grade levels, they report the score in terms of chronological years. The score is separated by a hyphen between the years and months and is based on the calendar year, not the school year. Therefore, a score of 7-6 (7 years-6 months) would reflect the performance of an average seven-and-one-half-year-old on that particular test.

These scores should also be reported as a range so that the 7-6 might have a Standard Error of Measurement of 0.2 (plus or minus) and be reported as 7-4 to 7-8. As is the case with grade equivalents, these scores should only be interpreted in the most general way.

Percentile Rank

This score demonstrates a student's relative position in a group of students who have taken a particular test. The percentile rank is the point below which the percentage of students register. For example, if a raw score on a spelling achievement test is 23, the information is not useful. Yet, when converted to a percentile rank of 67, for example, it means that the student performed better than 67 percent of the students taking the test at that time, or that 33 percent of the students taking the test at that time scored higher than that student.

Stanines

A stanine is obtained by dividing the raw test score into nine equal parts. For example, a student achieving a stanine score of 1 would be at the lowest end of the performance scale and a student with a stanine score of 9 would be at the highest, while a stanine score of 5 indicates the student percentile is exactly in the middle of the scores. Many tests report stanines, as well as one or more of the scores above.

Stanines are just another way to divide scores into units.

Limitations of Standardized Tests

When employed in conjunction with teacher-made tests, anecdotal reports, report cards, and ongoing observation in the classroom, standardized test results can contribute to the total picture of how well a student is performing in school. If they are used as a sole criteria to interpret a student's performance, however, then they are obstacles to effective instruction.

If you are concerned about the results of your child's testing, follow these steps:

Step 1. You will usually receive test information at a parent-teacher conference at the elementary level and through the mail at the secondary level. After receiving this information, request a total picture of your child; you should not be handed only the test score.

Talk to the teachers or guidance counselor about the relationship between the test scores and other evaluations of your child's performance. Is there consistency? Does each teacher or guidance counselor believe that the tests are accurate (valid/reliable) in your child's case?

In most circumstances, test scores represent only a part of your child's total performance. If you believe that the test scores are not an accurate measure of how your child performs in school, proceed to step 2.

Step 2. If the scores being presented are not a range of scores, insist on receiving a range. When given this range, you may decide that the discrepancy is not an issue.

Step 3. If a placement decision is being made based on the test scores and you are not in agreement, you have a number of options:

- Find out as much as you can about the particular test by contacting school personnel or calling a local college or university and inquiring about it from a member of the psychology or education department.
- Specifically ask: How reliable and valid is the test? What was the norming sample? What is the test's purpose? How should it be used?
- Ask the school to administer an individual test to provide you and the school with additional information.
- Obtain a second opinion from a college or university or hospital educational clinic. In this way you will be provided with a battery of individually administered tests that may help you make a more informed decision.
- Most schools have an appeals process in these matters. Find out the steps you must follow and speak to the appropriate school personnel.

Parents of special education children need to be vigilant about all aspects of their child's education. Considering the weight placed on standardized tests in our schools, parents should be aware that this is one area of critical importance.

32

~~~

UNDERSTANDING EDUCATIONESE

Aspecial language that we have named *educationese*, terms and jargon specifically related to the teaching profession, exists in today's schools. Many parents, because they are not familiar with this special language, may feel embarrassed about their lack of knowledge or understanding of a particular term used by school personnel. More problematic are situations in which parents make decisions for children based on a program or teaching system that is foreign to them.

Although the compilation of frequently used terms provided below is not exhaustive, it should be thorough enough to assist parents in most interactions with school personnel.

Elementary Grades
- **Basal readers.** A series of books based on a particular grade level used by the average reader. Typically, these readers incorporate a variety of reading approaches instead of utilizing one approach throughout. A student typically has a reader and workbook.
- **Child study team.** A group consisting of a psychologist, social worker, guidance counselor, classroom teacher, and principal who regularly meet to discuss ways to assist students at a risk. Team membership may vary from school to school.
- **Cultural literacy.** A body of knowledge that should be known by all who are literate in a particular culture. For

example, when television news reporters mention the Middle East, they assume that viewers understand that they are referring to the area of the world that includes Israel, Saudi Arabia, and Iraq.

- **Drill.** The repetition of basic skills to a point that they become automatic.
- **Dyslexia.** A general term used to refer to a language-based reading disorder which appears to stem from a central nervous system dysfunction. Parents need to know that this term is often used to describe any kind of reading problem. If it is suggested that a child has a reading disorder, his parents should consult with a learning disability or reading specialist.
- **Extended day.** A period of time beyond the traditional half-day kindergarten. For example, some school districts use this term to describe a full kindergarten day, while others use it to label an hour or so of kindergarten that is scheduled to extend a half-day kindergarten program.
- **Fine motor skills.** The skills that involve the body's small muscles; tasks such as handwriting, cutting, coloring, and drawing all require adequate fine motor skills.
- **Gifted/talented.** A program for a student who excels in a particular area of schooling.
- **Gross motor skills.** The skills that involve the body's large muscles. Physical activities such as throwing, running, and jumping, as well as general movement, are included in this group of skills.
- **Grouping by ability.** The act of dividing students into groups, such as reading or math, based on their abilities. This usually is based on test scores, teacher judgment and grades.
- **Mainstreaming.** The act of educating special education students in classes with their nondisabled peers.
- **Open classroom.** A nonstructured, flexible approach to

learning in which instruction is guided by the teacher, yet each child can progress at his own rate. An open class-room is more student-directed than a traditional class-room, which is more teacher-directed.

- **Phonics.** An approach to reading and spelling that teaches a student to associate letters with sounds. A student then uses these skills to analyze the sequence of sounds, put them together and pronounce new words.

- **Positive reinforcement.** The act of focusing on a student's appropriate behaviors and following that behavior with something positive, such as praise, a smile, a pat on the back, or a tangible reward.

- **Pull-out program.** A program that removes a student from his regular classroom so that he may receive instruction in a particular area by trained personnel. Remedial reading, resource rooms, speech therapy, and math labs are all examples of pull-out programs.

- **Readiness skills.** The skills that are deemed to be prerequisites for higher-level skills. For example, in order for a child to write, he must possess adequate eye-hand coordination and fine motor skills, as well as the ability to attend to a task.

- **Remedial reading/math.** Instruction given to a student when he falls below a certain level. A teacher with specific training in this area provides the instruction, usually on a short-term basis. Remedial instruction is not equivalent to special education.

- **Rote learning.** Learning that requires little thought process other than the memorization of a body of knowledge, such as a multiplication table or the names of planets.

- **Standardized tests.** Tests employed by school districts for a variety of reasons, including class grouping, course selection, reading groups, special education referrals, and program evaluations. These tests attempt to compare an individual child to a group of children who have taken the same test. Findings are reported in terms of a particular score, such as a grade level or an age level.

- **Support services.** Services that provide additional support beyond the classroom. These may include counseling, speech/language therapy, remediation, social work services, and parent training.
- **Tracking.** The act of placing students in the same grade in different learning groups, such as a lower track or a higher track, based on level of performance. In tracking, the groups are less fluid than when grouped by ability. Frequently, a student remains in a track throughout his school career. The notion of locking children into a certain level of classes has been criticized by some professionals.
- **Whole language approach.** An approach that emphasizes the language basis of listening, reading, speaking and writing, not rote learning. It is a natural, meaningful, thought out approach to language arts instruction. A student is immersed in literature and learns to develop an appreciation of it early in his school career.
- **Whole word ("look-say") approach.** An approach in which a student is taught to recall what a whole word looks like in order to read it, as opposed to using phonetic skills to sound the word out. The shapes of words are highlighted to help a student distinguish and remember them.

Middle/Junior High School
- **Accelerated class.** A class that allows a student to take two years' worth of course work in one year so that she can move more rapidly through her subjects. By the time a student enters high school, she may have already taken a few freshman level courses if she has taken accelerated classes.

- **Aptitude tests.** Tests that attempt to assess a student's ability to perform in specific areas. Schools usually administer aptitude tests in eighth grade to assist a student in planning his high school curriculum and career possibilities.
- **Content area.** A specific body of knowledge that is distinguished from the basic skill subjects of reading, writing, and math. However, a content area, such as social studies, French, or geometry, utilizes the basic skill subjects.
- **Extracurricular activities.** Activities beyond the traditional school curriculum. Although some extracurricular activities may have existed in elementary school, the options available in junior high school are more abundant and varied. Activities include athletics, speech/drama clubs and student government, for example.
- **Guidance counselor.** A counselor who will assist a student in course selection, help develop her high school curriculum and, depending upon the administrator's training, advise her on other education-related matters.
- **Interdisciplinary studies.** Studies that combine two or more subjects, such as English and science, so that a student can apply one content area to other subjects. For example, a student can apply his writing skills in the area of science and his scientific inquiry skills in English. Depending on the creativity of the teacher(s) involved, there are any number of possibilities for interdisciplinary studies.
- **Peer pressure.** The pressure exerted on a student to be part of a group. At the middle/junior high school level, a particularly strong pull exists for a student to be like his friends. Conforming, therefore, in terms of dress, language, and behavior standards, is deemed important by a student. While most aspects of peer pressure are not harmful, responding to pressure from peers to act

inappropriately may cause a student to adopt troublemaking behavior in and out of school.

- **Progress reports.** Reports issued between report cards to inform a student and his parents of his performance. Although many schools still only send "poor" progress reports, more are realizing the importance of informing a child and his parents that the young pupil is performing well.

High School

- **Advanced placement.** Classes that enable a student to take a test (referred to as an AP test) that may enable him to receive advanced placement for college courses. Some colleges will actually give credit hours depending on the student's test results, while others will waive specific courses.
- **American College Test (ACT).** A standardized test, including English and math usage; social studies comprehension; and natural science reading. These test results are used as one selection criteria for college admission.
- **Career education.** Exposure to the various occupations that are available in the work world. While this should be provided throughout a student's school career, it is often not until high school that he receives such exposure.
- **Electives.** Courses that are not required. A student should select his electives with care, because more often than not, the many course requirements imposed on high school students do not leave many open hours in which electives may be scheduled.
- **Graduation requirements.** Specific requirements, such as grades or standardized tests, for a student to complete successfully in order to graduate. A student and his parents should be aware of their state's requirements early in the child's high school career so that they can be certain

that he is proceeding according to an appropriate academic sequence.

- **Honors classes.** Classes that provide opportunities for more in-depth exploration of a topic than traditional classes. A student is selected for these classes; the criteria upon which the selection is based vary.
- **PSAT.** A standardized test that is viewed as a practice test for the SAT I. This test usually is taken in the latter half of the tenth grade or in the beginning of the eleventh grade.
- **SAT I.** A standardized test taken during the junior or senior year of high school, or both years, that is used as one indicator of a student's ability to succeed in college. It measures quantitative and verbal skills.
- **Vocational education.** Training in a particular vocational area for a student who does not wish to pursue a college education. Some high schools are equipped to provide vocational education, while others contract with outside agencies for these types of classes.

Part Five

~~~~~~

EXTRACURRICULAR ACTIVITIES FOR CHILDREN WITH ADD

C hildren with ADD can benefit greatly from extracurricular activities. The following Keys will present guidelines for involvement in sports, clubs, camps, hobbies, and special talent or interest groups.

33

SPORTS AND CLUBS

I t would be natural for parents to believe that sports would be an ideal activity for their children because it would provide them with opportunities to expend excessive energy. However, it's not so simple. It is important to recognize that some children with ADD will never work off their excessive energy. True, there are times when they become tired, but there is also the possibility that their high energy level can be increased by too much stimulation. This overstimulation can lead to more impulsive, distractible and, in some cases, aggressive behavior. There is also the issue of focusing on relevant information. Sports, both individual and group, require a great deal of concentration. The rules of baseball, for example, can be complicated for a child who has a hard time listening and attending, especially on a large field with numerous distractions. In addition to the rules there is a new vocabulary to contend with. A youngster told one of us during a basketball game, "Just stop talking and shoot!"

Participation in sports must be well thought out and planned. It's a good idea to get children involved in a sport when they are younger because the rules are simplified and the competition is less severe. Also, during the early years there is much more variability in skill level, so that your child will have ample opportunity to learn the basics of a sport. In addition, there is usually far greater opportunity to practice during this age.

Before enrolling in a sport, it is crucial that you speak to the coach. It is helpful to explain the nature of your child's particular attention deficit to the coach, providing examples of the way it might be manifested in this sport. Many parents have done this and have been successful. Initially, some were reluctant because they thought it would predispose the coach to treat their child differently. They soon came to realize that the nature of ADD is such that it would be apparent in a short period of time that their child has a hard time focusing and is often distractible and hyperactive. Rather than have the coach attribute this behavior to other factors, it's good to speak to the coach before any participation. You may also want to share some things that you do that are successful in dealing with your child's behavior. It is important to realize that most coaches truly care for children—often volunteering enumerable hours—and are willing to help out when parents provide them with adequate information.

The first experiences with sports should be positive. Start with a sport that is simple to follow and allows for ample practice, for example, soccer before the age of eight. The major components of ADD—distractibility, impulsivity, and hyperactivity—may make it difficult for your child to participate in some sports. Sports are much more than opportunities to "burn off steam." The attention to important rules and regulations may frustrate some children and increased physical activity may serve to exacerbate the hyperactive behavior.

Sports can provide wonderful experiences for physical activity and social interaction if they are appropriate for the child or adolescent with ADD. Parents need to consider the behaviors their child displays and the demands of a particular sport and decide if it is a "good fit."

145

Sports are not the only extracurricular activity that children with ADD can get involved in. There is a wide variety of clubs that can also provide your child with a wealth of experiences. Some clubs are typically associated with schools, such as community-service clubs, science clubs, environment clubs, and math clubs. Usually these clubs are for students who display an interest in these areas, not necessarily a degree of excellence. Other clubs are more community based, such as 4-H, Cub Scouts, Brownies, Girl Scouts, and Boy Scouts.

The type of club and level of participation cannot be left to chance. When you are deciding upon a particular club, discuss the types of activities the kids typically engage in. Are they of interest to your child? Find out how many children are enrolled in the club. The Cub Scouts may sound like a wonderful notion, but the groups may be too large for your child. Inquire about the rules and regulations of the club. In some clubs the rules are so extensive that they would challenge any child, not to mention a child with ADD. Some clubs spend a lot of time lecturing, while others have greater opportunities for hands-on activities. Once you have narrowed down your choices, have your child attend a meeting on a trial basis in order to see if she enjoys the club. The final deciding factor will be the leader. You should feel comfortable not only with his expertise, but the manner in which he treats children. Go with your instincts if you feel good about him. Provide him with adequate information so that he will understand the nature of your child's ADD. Give him a few effective techniques for dealing with your child.

Some clubs are geared specifically for children with special needs. For example, there are Brownie, Cub Scout, Boy Scout and Girl Scout groups that serve students with learning disabilities. The decision to join such an organization should be based on a number of variables, the most prominent being what other disabilities are concomitant with ADD. Generally speaking, most children with ADD can be appropriately accommodated in a club for nondisabled children. For those who cannot, it is fortunate that we have specialized groups.

A word of caution: Sports activities and clubs are appealing to children and adolescents. We've known of some children with ADD who would sign up for every club if given the opportunity. It is up to parents to decide what is an appropriate allocation of time for clubs in their child's schedule. Otherwise, your child may become overloaded and not enjoy the benefits of participating in these activities. When looking at organizations, parents should look for ones that are well structured, relatively small, noncompetitive, and pleasurable.

34

CAMPS

School vacations, in particular the long, hot summer, are particularly troublesome for children with ADD and for their families. Students may find it difficult to adjust from the predictable structure of the school day. The lack of structure and academic demands are a few of the benefits of a school vacation, but for many this just leads to restlessness and chaos. Camps can fill the void.

Day Camp

A good day camp can provide a structured, reinforcing day that enables a child or adolescent to develop her strengths. There may be concern for the length of the day. It is long and when you add in transportation to and from camp it's small wonder that many kids appear to be in a stupor as they emerge from the bus. However, it is a well-organized, structured day with a variety of activities. Frequently, teachers from local schools are employed as counselors and are somewhat knowledgeable of the needs of children with ADD. Camp directors are usually very amenable to parental input.

Start your search for a camp early in the year. Camps are frequently listed in local and national newspapers, in particular, newspapers and magazines geared towards parents. You should be alert to camp fairs, typically held in January or February, which allow you to find out about a large number of camps in one day. Also, speak to your child's teacher to see if she can recommend a camp. And finally, speak to parents of children with ADD in order to find out what their experiences have been with local day camps.

Sleep-away Camps

If your child is older and has become tired of day camps you may be interested in sleep-away camps. Since your child will be away from home for at least two weeks and usually much more, ask yourself the following questions: Has your child been away from home for any extended period of time? How does your child respond to authority figures? Does she make friends easily? Your responses will help you to decide whether a sleep-away camp is appropriate for your child. There are camps geared specifically for children with ADD. This type of camp may be a good idea for those children or adolescents with severe attention deficits. However, you should investigate the camp thoroughly. ADD is a term that is used very casually in some circles and you need to clarify the specific population the camp is serving. It may be markedly different from your child.

Camps affiliated with a club your child belongs to or a religious organization would be a particularly good choice in that they would be familiar with your child and vice versa. The transition from home to camp would be eased by this familiarity. The first camp experience should be relatively short (two weeks) and the subsequent stays should depend on your child's success.

If you are considering a camp, familiarize yourself with the list of suggestions provided by Resources for Children with Special Needs, Inc. (New York, NY):

SUGGESTIONS FOR SELECTING A CAMP

A summer spent at a day camp, sleep-away camp, or travel camp should be a productive living and learning experience. It can be fun, healthy, and can provide an opportunity to develop new skills and friendships. A camp experience may have a great impact on a child's life, so it is important for parents and caregivers to make a careful decision in choosing a camp. Not every camp meets the needs and abilities of every child.

Since you are the consumer, you have a right to ask any question you wish so that you can better understand the camp program. Some of the questions you may want to consider are listed below.

You and Your Child
- What do you want out of your child's camp experience? Improvement in specific areas (language, reading, gross motor skills, social interaction, skills of daily living, etc.)?
- What does your child want out of his/her camp experience? A good time? New friends? New skills?
- Is your child ready for a day camp?
- Is your child ready for a sleep-away camp?
- Has your child spent time away from home overnight at a friend's or relative's home?

Director and Staff
- Who is the director? What are his/her qualifications?
- What are the qualifications of the staff members (education, age, training)? How are they supervised?
- What is the professional staff to camper ratio (senior counselors, waterfront staff, therapists, medical personnel)?
- Who are the medical staff (Doctor, nurse...)?
- What is the percentage of returning staff?
- What kind of screening process is used to select staff?

Camp Program
- What is a typical day like? What are the activities? Do children have a choice of activities?

- Is one-to-one instruction provided for some activities?
- How is the waterfront program run? What are the qualifications of the waterfront staff? What are the safety procedures? How often do children swim?
- Are activities varied for different age groups?
- What do children do on a rainy day? Do they stay in camp or go to other facilities?
- What is the range of abilities and special needs of the campers?
- How does the program meet individual needs and differences?
- How are behavior problems handled?
- What is done to deal with a child's fear or resistance to a particular activity, i.e., swimming, horseback riding, boating?
- What is the percentage of returning campers?
- What procedure exists for medical emergencies?
- What is the overall philosophy of the camp? (Goals for the children.)

Camp Setting

- What is the overall appearance of the campsite?
- What are the facilities like for indoor and outdoor sports and games? If applicable, are they accessible for children with physical disabilities?
- Where are the kitchen and dining areas? Do campers and staff eat together? Are provisions made for special dietary needs?
- Are buildings and equipment safe, well-lighted and in good repair?
- Do children sleep in tents? Cabins? Where are bathroom and shower facilities? Are they kept in sanitary condition?
- Is there plenty of equipment in good condition?
- How many counselors live in each of the cabins or bunks?

Other Things to Consider

- What is a typical menu? Who prepares the food?
- What medical facilities are available at the camp?
- Are there procedures for the administration of medication?
- What procedures are in place for medical emergencies? How does your child get to the campsite? (Transportation provided?)
- Do staff members speak other languages?
- Is there a visitors' day for parents? Are parents able to arrange a visit other than on visitors' day? Are parents able to call?
- How is information concerning children's progress shared with parents and/or schools after the camp season?
- What can you as the parent share with the camp that will be helpful?
- What system exists for laundering of clothing?
- Do you want your child to be mainstreamed with non-disabled children for all or part of the day?
- What options does the camp offer pertaining to payment (scholarship, sliding scale, payment plans)?

35

HOBBIES AND SPECIAL TALENTS/INTERESTS

One of the wonderful things about hobbies is that children and adolescents can become "experts." This is particularly beneficial for students with ADD. Often the feedback they receive from parents, teachers, and classmates is negative. Coupled with their difficulty in establishing meaningful social relationships, this negative feedback can lower their self-esteem. By developing a hobby they can acquire knowledge and skills for which they are perceived as competent, as an "expert" in one particular area of interest.

Hobbies don't just emerge, they must be fostered. Parents must expose their children to a wide variety of experiences and reinforce their interests. In addition to trips to the zoo, museums, aquariums, historical sites, and the like, parents can foster hobbies by enrolling children in courses related to their interests or providing them with unusual experiences. Many communities have arts and crafts classes, music classes, gymnastics, and so forth. Museums and philharmonic orchestras frequently have programs specifically geared towards youngsters. Many of these are appropriate for children with ADD because they are relatively short and are only scheduled on a weekly basis, hence the novelty of the activity tends to capture their attention. As with sports and clubs, you need to assess the expectation of the teachers of these classes and the number of students who participate.

Beyond these hobbies there are many more to be discovered if you have the time and inclination to explore. Children have developed interests in such activities as illustrating, Morse code, and miniature furniture. Collections in stamps, coins, baseball cards, and rocks capture the imagination of many children. The list is endless. All that is necessary is enthusiasm and time. It may take a while before you find a hobby that truly interests your child, so don't give up. It is exciting to see a child develop a hobby to a point where others solicit their advice. We recall the look of pride on one youngster's face when an adult asked him about the value of a particular baseball card. He seemed amazed and proud that he knew more about this topic than even his teacher. A hobby can develop a unique competence that is often hard to find in school or extracurricular activities.

If you find it impossible to come up with a hobby that is of interest to your child you may want to ask her teacher. There are many different activities that children engage in during a school day. Perhaps the teacher has noticed your child's particular interest in one of them, one in which she has demonstrated some competence. Also check with the special subject teachers, that is, art, music, physical education, and computers. Their expertise in a particular field may enable them to identify some activity that could lead to further exploration. Although it is not critical that your child have a hobby, it can do wonders for her self-esteem.

Extracurricular activities are important for children with ADD. The sports they play, the hobbies they develop, the camps they attend all help to round out children, to make them more than merely persons who have difficulty paying attention in school. Although the term *extracurricular* suggests something that is beyond school, these activities are an integral part of the learning process. Frequently such activities can be employed to enhance attention and to reinforce desired behavior.

Perhaps even more important than encouraging these types of activities is the nurturing of a special talent a child may possess. Because of the behavioral problems associated with ADD, it may be difficult for parents to identify a special talent. You might solicit the input of teachers or, if your child has been enrolled in classes such as art, gymnastics, or the like, you might inquire about exploring higher level or enrichment courses in an area in which your child demonstrates particular talent. For example, we know of a child who has been diagnosed as having ADD and has considerable difficulty staying on task in school. He happened to be enrolled in a weekend class that dealt with the environment, during which the instructor noticed a particular talent in science. The instructor informed the parents and the child has been enrolled in a number of classes outside of the school that reinforce this particular ability. Additionally, his parents make frequent trips to the local science museum, read books related to science to him, and have hired a science teacher to work with him one hour per week to expand upon his interest and talents. Over the years, this special talent has manifested itself in many ways and he has become extremely competent, some would say "gifted," in this important area of the curriculum. It is with a tremendous sense of pride that he answers the questions of adults, knowing that they seek him out for his special talent. There are other examples in the arts, music, technology, and sports that children and adolescents with ADD have demonstrated special talents.

The common thread through these examples is the commitment of the parents. It takes an extraordinary amount of time and energy to travel to special places, to seek special events, to balance the special talent with other activities, but it is necessary if the talents are to emerge. We know a youngster who is an exceptionally good gymnast. She has far exceeded the skills level of her local gymnastic class so her parents drive her (three times per week) to a special gymnastic academy in order for her to further develop this talent. It would be easier to ignore such a talent, especially since her behavioral disorders related to ADD continue to cause concerns at school. However, the parents' willingness and ability to continue having this extra training has enabled this youngster to excel, and others have come to view her as extremely talented in this area and treat her with awe. This attention can go a long way when she is reprimanded for being fidgety in school.

Not all children with ADD have special talents. In reality, not many of us have such gifts. However, if talents are present they should be encouraged and enhanced. A child should never be pressured or forced to excel. Typically, if you expose your child to a wide variety of activities at an early age she will have many opportunities for hobbies to develop. If in your opinion and that of professionals involved in the activity your child is deemed to have a special talent, then we encourage you to pursue it.

Part Six

~~~~~~

CURRENT ISSUES

There are many issues that are currently being discussed about ADD. The following keys will focus on these questions:

- Is ADD a learning disability?
- Is ADD a special education classification?
- Are children with ADD receiving appropriate treatment in school settings?
- Do children outgrow ADD?
- Is ADD restricted to boys?

36

IS ADD A LEARNING DISABILITY?

Public Law 94-142 (The Education of the Handicapped Act of 1975) defines *specific learning disabilities* as

a disorder in one or more of the basic psychological processes involved in understanding or in using language, spoken or written, which may manifest itself in an imperfect ability to listen, think, speak, read, write, spell, or to do mathematical calculations. The term includes such conditions as perceptual handicaps, brain injury, minimal brain dysfunction, dyslexia, and developmental aphasia. The term does not include children who have learning problems which are primarily the result of visual, hearing, or motor handicaps, or mental retardation, of emotional disturbance, or of environmental, cultural, or economic disadvantage.

This definition is used in schools throughout the country. Many experts disagree, not only on the definition of learning disability (LD), but also on the identification procedures, incidence figures of children with learning disabilities, and remedial procedures. This is important to note because it is not a simple matter to diagnose and to treat learning disabilities. The link that appears to exist between LD and ADD is related to characteristics used to describe LD students.

They are frequently described as being hyperactive, impulsive, and distractible. In fact, when teachers are asked to characterize LD students, they list short attention span and hyperactivity as the first two characteristics. It should not be surprising, therefore, that many people think that the terms are synonymous. They are not. There are other characteristics associated with LD, such as disorders of memory and thinking, disorders of language, perceptual disorders, specific academic disabilities (reading, writing, spelling, arithmetic) as well as social perceptual problems. And although some LD students clearly have problems with attention and are hyperactive, impulsive, and distractible, many are not.

Some psychologists and educators have suggested that a learning disability can cause an ADD. The thinking on this subject is that poor school performance can cause frustration that leads to hyperactive behavior. There are many students who are hyperactive because they are anxious. A child who is doing poorly in school may be anxious or perhaps depressed. But this is not the hyperactivity one associates with ADD. The former is more environmentally produced, whereas the latter is a neurologically based disorder. A learning disability, therefore, could not cause ADD, because ADD is a disorder whose etiology is an interaction of biological and psychological difficulties.

Another question that has been asked is whether or not ADD can cause an LD. The answer is no. A learning disability is a neurologically based disorder and, although an ADD can coexist with an LD it cannot cause it. A child with an undiagnosed ADD will have trouble in school. Once diagnosed and properly treated, however, the school performance should be fine. If it is not, the reason may be something other than a learning disability. This is a controversial issue and not all professionals agree with this response.

Finally, are there children who have both a learning disability and an attention deficit disorder? The answer is yes. According to the professional literature, there appears to be a group of students who overlap both categories. While the figure varies from study to study, it appears to be about a third of each population. It may be helpful to conceptualize it by using the diagram below:

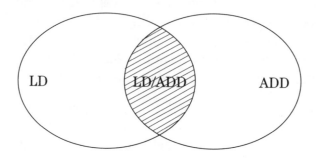

The shaded area represents the group of students who have learning disabilities and ADD. As the diagram shows, however, most children with LD do not have ADD, nor do most children with ADD have learning disabilities.

The issue of LD and ADD is not a minor one. Our major concern is related to treatment. It is easy to understand why parents of children with ADD may think that their child has a learning disability, because ADD is an incredibly misunderstood term and often used too casually. However, as the definition above cites, LD refers to a specific group (although heterogeneous) of people (probably around 3-5%) who are experiencing school failure due to a neurological disorder that effects basic psychological processes. ADD is also a neurological disorder, but it manifests itself in hyperactive, impulsive, and distractible behavior. Therefore, to treat each group of children in the same manner would be inappropriate. For example, to place a child with ADD in a resource room for special education students without any intervention for the attentional problems would be ineffective. Equally ineffective would be to place an LD student on medication and provide him with behavioral intervention and counseling without any academic remediation. The treatment depends upon the diagnosis; if the diagnosis is incorrect then it follows that the treatment will also be incorrect.

There is also one more issue central to this question; that is the provision of services for children with ADD. Although LD is a relatively new diagnostic category, it is recognized in P.L. 94-142 as a "specific handicapping condition." Many parents of children with ADD feel that they are not receiving the services they would if these disorders were classified as LD. This issue will be addressed in the following Keys. For additional information see *Keys to Parenting a Child with a Learning Disability,* by Barry and Francine McNamara (Barron's).

37

~~~~~~

IS ADD A SPECIAL EDUCATION CLASSIFICATION?

Whether or not children diagnosed as having ADD should be classified as students with special educational needs and receive special education services has been a fiercely debated controversy. On one side were parents and professionals who argued that ADD is a specific condition and that children and adolescents with ADD were not receiving appropriate educational services. On the other side were those who felt that children and adolescents with ADD could receive special education services provided under existing categories, such as learning disabilities, emotional disturbance, or other health impaired; therefore, a new classification was unnecessary.

At the core of the controversy is the provision of services for students with ADD. Recent legislative action has added some clarity to the situation. The Individuals with Disabilities Education Act (IDEA) which was passed in October of 1990, reauthorized Public Law 94-142, Education of the Handicapped Act. During the debate on IDEA, the question of a separate disability for ADD arose. After considerable public hearings and discussion, the U.S. Department of Education issued a Policy Memorandum in September of 1991 that finally recognized ADD as a disability under IDEA.

That is, it is considered a disability and can be diagnosed and treated under other classifications (Learning Disabilities, Emotional Disorders, or other Health Impairments.)

What does all of this mean for parents of children with ADD? It means that their children can receive special education and related services (such as speech, adaptive physical education, and others) when the ADD impairs their ability to perform in school. It did not establish ADD as a separate category because it was felt that these children could receive services under the existing categories, most likely learning disabilities (LD) or emotional disorders (ED). If the major disability is ADD, students are eligible for special education and related services under the category of Other Health Impaired. What this means is that even if your child does not meet the criteria for LD, he can be recognized and served under the law (IDEA). This does not satisfy everybody, but it is a step toward the recognition of a complex disorder.

A child with ADD is also recognized under Section 504 of the Rehabilitation Act of 1973, which insures the civil and constitutional rights of individuals with disabilities. At first, schools were not covered, but in 1978 the law was changed so that children with ADD could receive assistance in schools if their disability (ADD) substantially limits their ability to learn or to otherwise benefit from their educational program. Types of assistance may include the training of regular educators to enable them to be more effective with students with ADD, simplification of the curriculum, behavioral interventions—whatever is necessary to accommodate the student with ADD.

This does not mean that the controversy is over. There was considerable disagreement on the responses to the questions about ADD for the Department of Education Public

Hearings. The summary of the hearings is over 200 pages. What follows is a synopsis of the hearings put together by Mary Fowler, CHADD, Governmental Affairs Committee Chairperson.

Question A: *Are children with ADD...currently being excluded from special education programs ... to what extent and what are the reasons for such exclusions?*

1165 responses—Mostly from parents who reported their children were excluded or receiving inappropriate programs. Numerous other respondents said children with ADD were not excluded if they had a co-existing disability. Some said regular education should be able to address ADD problems. Some said ADD was already served under other health impaired. Others reported that they could not determine service delivery since ADD is not counted in and of itself. One parent wrote, "Ethan has been isolated in the classroom and 'because you can't behave.' he has been given a rubber spider for being the most unusual student, he has been barred from social activities in his school because he can't sit in his seat or keep his hands from moving."

Question B: *To what extent are children with ADD... currently being identified within existing disability categories in part B, such as "other health impaired," "seriously emotionally disturbed," or "specific learning disability"?*

827 responses—Many commenters indicated children with ADD qualify for special education and related services within existing disability categories. The three disability categories mentioned almost exclusively are specific learning disability, seriously emotionally disturbed, and other health impaired in this order of frequency. Other respondents reported that current categories are not sufficient for appro-

priate identification and service and that ADD is not addressed within them. Some respondents said they "stretched" eligibility criteria to include children with ADD.

Question C: *Do children with ADD have unique characteristics that are not reflected in the existing disability categories in part B? If so, to what extent do these unique characteristics require separate evaluation criteria, special preparation for instructional and support personnel and distinct educational programs and services?*

1168 responses—Numerous commenters said ADD had unique characteristics that are not reflected in existing disability categories. Some respondents indicated that ADD was a medical problem controlled through medication. Opinions varied on whether separate evaluation criteria are needed, but numerous commenters said "training in characteristics of ADD and the appropriate instructional interventions must be comprehensive and must be directed toward both instructional and administrative personnel....Many commenters added that the training provided should be mandatory."

One administrator wrote, "ADD has become a 'hot topic,' a 'buzz word,' and to some parents there is some status if your child has this diagnosis" (Maybe we should send this respondent all of our children for a weekend.) A teacher wrote, "We know that our students need our help and guidance but often we are at a loss for knowing what to do. My educational preparation at the university level was extremely lacking with regard to education of students with any type of special need... The current assessment tools which are used to evaluate most students referred for evaluation are not sensitive to the disability areas of ADD children."

Question D: *What educational programs and/or services are school districts currently providing to children* *diagnosed as having ADD, either in special education programs or in general education?*

786 responses—"Depending on the severity of the disorder, a child may receive services in the regular education classroom, a resource room setting, self-contained classroom, or special school... The severity of the ADD appears to provide a reference point for the delivery of services, as well as the absence or presence of a coexisting disability." Most comments said ADD children could be served in regular education with trained teachers. No specific programs were mentioned.

Question E: *How should ADD be described operationally for purposes of qualifying a child for special education and related services under part B?*

607 responses—Many commenters suggested using *DSM* criteria in conjunction with specific criterion to assess discrepancy between academic performance and ability. Many respondents said ADD should not be included as a disability category. An administrator wrote, "The definition should also require several attempts to control the disorder through the use of medication and should eliminate from consideration those disorders that are successfully controlled by the use of medication." A respondent categorized as "other" wrote, "Under no circumstances shall a student with ADD have his or her right to a free and appropriate public education conditioned upon his or her taking medication as a course of treatment for ADD."

The National School Board Association wrote, "There is no consensus regarding an appropriate definition of ADD. Behaviors that characterize ADD in most cases are indistinguishable from behaviors that any child exhibits at some time or to some degree or that can be associated with the socio-economic condition of the child. In addition, there is not an accepted standard as to the degree to which these behaviors must be exhibited to identify a child as having ADD..."

Question F: *What criteria should be included in the definition to qualify children with ADD...to be eligible for special education and related services under part B?*

541 responses —"The manifestations of ADD frequently mentioned throughout the comments received include inattentiveness, distractibility, hyperactivity, impulsivity, excessive motor activity, oppositional behavior, inability to focus, and lack of organizational skills. Many commenters stressed that ADD must adversely affect the child's ability to perform successfully in school."

Question G: *What specific manifestation of ADD, if any, should be included in the definition?*

530 responses—Specific manifestations frequently mentioned throughout the comments are the same as those mentioned in Question F and listed above.

Question H: *Should the definition include references to characteristics or circumstances that produce transient inattentive behaviors, that in and of themselves, would not make a child eligible for special education and related services under the definition attention deficit disorder?*

521 responses—The majority of respondents answered "yes" to this question.

Question I: *Should the definition address the concurrence of ADD with other disabilities, such as specific learning disabilities or serious emotional disturbance, and if so addressed, how should this be accomplished?*

520 responses—Many said concurrence should be recognized. Several commenters said the assessment should be comprehensive and "should identify all disabilities in order that appropriate interventions can be designed to address each child's needs." One commenter wrote that when concurrent disabling conditions exist, "the diagnostic entity that most interferes with the child's development should be listed as the primary condition."

Question J: *Should the definition address the concurrence of ADD with other disabilities, such as specific learning disabilities or serious emotional disturbance, and if so addressed, how should this be accomplished?*

578 responses—Those who said guidelines should be provided emphasized the need for uniformity. Those who said guidelines should not be provided felt that ADD should not be considered as a disability category or that ADD was identified under existing guidelines. NASDE (National Association of State Directors of Special Education) wrote, "Guidelines setting forth explicit criteria and standards regarding evaluations of children suspected of having ADD should be immediately issued to state and local educational agencies. The symptoms of ADD and the sophistication therefore required for accurate assessment (see, e.g., PGARD response to items f, j, and l of this notice of inquiry) make this a critical safeguard against misclassification."

Question K: *Who should be authorized to conduct an assessment of a child having or suspected of having attention deficit disorder, and should the assessment be conducted by more than one individual (such as a teacher and a psychologist)?*

683 responses—Several commenters said only a physician should conduct the assessment for ADD. Others indi-

cated educators. Many said a multidisciplinary approach should be used which included both medical and educational assessments. Others said educators could be trained to verify that a child has ADD and then to assess the impact of ADD on educational performance.

Question L: *What provision should be included in the definition, and what additional steps, if any, should be included to ensure that children who are from racial, ethnic, and linguistic minorities are not misclassified under this definition?*

470 responses—Several suggestions offered included use of multiple information sources, assurances that other educational methods had been exhausted, and training of those who would be responsible for the assessment. The Department concluded the report by including excerpts from many of the responses it had received. The following response from a teacher sums up why CHADD felt it necessary to take our issue to Washington. "Perhaps this is a medical or 'regular ed' problem, as some would have us believe. The real owner of the problem is the child who has to live every day of his/her life with the stress of constantly trying to keep thoughts channeled, body seated, the expectations of others prioritized and somehow met... This child is a VICTIM OF OUR BUREAUCRATIC NONSENSE AND CONTINUES TO FLOUNDER IN OUR INCOMPETENCE."

The Department of Education Memorandum and Section 504 of the Rehabilitation Act of 1973 provide the legislation necessary to get services for children with ADD. What remains to be seen is how schools will provide such services. Parents who approach school districts with concrete information regarding ADD are more likely to receive services for their children.

38

ARE CHILDREN WITH ADD RECEIVING APPROPRIATE TREATMENT?

Many parents and professionals believe children with ADD are not receiving appropriate services. They have argued that the existing categories are not sufficient to meet the needs of the ADD population. Recent legislation guarantees services to children with ADD, so we are hopeful that this will bring about a more reasonable and sensible approach to educating children with ADD.

It is necessary to look at the categories in which children with ADD would be placed: learning disabilities (LD), emotional disturbance (ED), and other health impaired (OHI).

Learning Disabilities

In order to be classified as learning disabled, a student must display a discrepancy between ability and achievement (see Key 31 for a more detailed discussion of these terms). Many children who have an ADD do not exhibit this discrepancy; therefore, they would not be eligible for services. Learning disabilities is a process disorder (how one listens, thinks, speaks, reads, writes) that may or may not manifest itself in hyperactivity, distractibility, or impulsivity. If those characteristics are not present, then classifying a child with ADD as LD will not be possible or appropriate.

Emotional Disorders

Many children with ADD have some type of behavioral problem in the classroom. The term *emotional disorders* is somewhat vague. Although it may include some of the problems experienced by children with ADD, it is also insufficient to meet the needs of many children with ADD. Parents are uncomfortable with the term because they believe their children are not emotionally disturbed and should not be grouped with children having all psychiatric and psychological problems. Also, teachers report that the behavioral problems experienced by children with ADD are different from those children who are truly emotionally disturbed.

Other Health Impaired

The last option for identifying and serving the needs of children with ADD is other health impaired (OHI). This classification is for students who require ongoing medical attention for conditions such as asthma, heart defects, cancer, and diabetes. Fortunately, there aren't many children classified as OHI (only twelve percent of the school-aged population) and within that number hardly any with ADD. Whether this category becomes a viable option remains to be seen. IDEA (97) specifically cited AD/HD as eligible for services under this classification.

The existing special education categories are not being used to meet the needs of children and adolescents with ADD. If the recent laws are properly implemented, this bleak picture may become a little brighter. Until that point we would support the following recommendation of Harvey Parker, Ph.D., founder of CHADD.

Educational Services Necessary for Students with ADD

Effective identification and management of the educational needs of ADD students require greater teacher education and awareness of the disorder, implementation of standardized screening and assessment techniques for identifying students with ADD, and application of proven educational and psychological strategies to teach and manage students with the disorder.

Training School Personnel

The majority of educators in this county have had little training in teaching students with ADD. Schools of education in colleges and universities have not provided instructional material on this disorder to properly train our nation's teachers. It is essential that programs be made available to educate school administrators, teachers, guidance personnel, and other school-based professionals about this disorder. Such programs could be delivered through in-service training, recertification courses, or added to already existing curricula within college and university settings. These programs should include topics such as:

1. Characteristics of students with ADD.
2. Methods of identifying students with ADD.
3. Etiology, treatment, and course of ADD.
4. Techniques and strategies for effectively teaching students with ADD.
5. Educational, psychological, and social needs of ADD students.
6. Understanding the family of ADD students.
7. Networking with physicians, mental health professionals, and parents to design and implement a multimodal treatment plan for the ADD student.

Assessment of Students' Needs

Providing direct services to students considered at risk for ADD should begin with proper assessment. This will likely require the coordinated efforts of a multimodal assessment team comprised of the members of a school's child study team (i.e., teachers, school psychologists, guidance counselors, exceptional student education specialists), input from medical specialists such as pediatricians, neurologists, or psychiatrists; and opinions of other health care professionals (i.e., clinical or educational psychologists, psychiatric social workers, mental health counselors, speech and language therapists, occupational or physical therapists) who may have evaluated the student. Since the average age of onset of ADD is within the preschool years, it is important that appropriate screening and referral procedures for early identification be established and that guidelines be set up to provide for identification of suspected students with ADD in all grades. The following points should be considered in the setting up of such procedures:

1. Standardized screening procedures for ADD should be available for preschool and kindergarten students who are identified as being at risk.
2. Once a student in any grade has been screened or identified by teachers and parents to be at risk for ADD, standardized procedures should be followed to provide for a comprehensive assessment. Such assessment procedures should make use of multiple sources of information about the student and should include:
   a. A general medical evaluation.
   b. A structured interview with the student's parents and teachers.
   c. Completion of behavior rating scales by the student's parents and teachers.

    d. Observation of the student's performance in the classroom.

    e. Assessment of the student's performance on tests of intelligence, cognitive processing, emotionality, and academic achievement.

    f. Assessment of the student's performance on tests specifically designed to measure sustained attention and impulsivity.

    g. Assessment of the student's speech, language, and fine and gross motor functioning when indicated.

Educational Programming Accommodations and Related Services

After the assessment, if it is determined that the student's classroom behavior and learning is significantly impaired as a result of having ADD, then appropriate recommendations should be made by the child study team that allow for the student to be classified as disabled on this basis and to receive any educational services deemed necessary by the team. This should occur even if the student's handicapping condition is solely due to the ADD without the co-existence of either a learning disability, severe emotional disturbance, or other heretofore recognized handicapping condition under P.L. 94-142. In such cases an Individualized Education Program (I.E.P.) should be developed with respect to the student's instructional programming. Such programming should be geared to each student's individual needs as identified in the comprehensive assessment.

The needs of many ADD students may be adequately served within the regular classroom as long as accommodations for the student's learning and behavioral difficulties are made. Such accommodations may involve the implementation of behavioral management programs, greater teacher supervision of the student, revised teacher expectations to account for the student's handicaps, the presence of a teacher's aide to assist with instruction. Placement of ADD students within the "least restrictive environment" guidelines should be followed. However, some ADD students with severe conditions may require placement in resource classrooms either part time or full time, or placement in day treatment or residential treatment programs. Periodic reevaluation of students' needs should be done with resulting redesign of the I.E.P. so as to take into account possible changes because of treatment effects, maturation, and other factors.

Auxiliary services will need to be developed because of the chronicity and severity associated with ADD. Such auxiliary services might include counseling for the child, social skills training, or occupational therapy. Furthermore, families of ADD students will require related services to assist them in their adjustment. Such related services should include participation in an ADD support group, individual or family education with respect to ADD, or involvement in family counseling.

39

~~~~~~

GIRLS WITH ADD

Some experts suggest that 80 percent of all individuals diagnosed with ADD are males. Does this mean that females truly represent such a small percentage or is it merely a case of underdiagnosis? Clearly, if you listen to parents of girls diagnosed with ADD or to women diagnosed with ADD, it is apparent that ADD is much more prevalent than the incidence figures would suggest. Oftentimes the girl who is dismissed as "spacey," "out of it," and "in the clouds" ends up having ADD.

There has been increased interest in females with ADD, and this Key will discuss some of the issues that are specific to girls with ADD. Dr. Kathleen Nadeau has written widely on this topic. She notes that in childhood many girls with ADD are hypersocial and hyper-emotional. Girls diagnosed with predominantly inattentive type of ADD may be very sensitive to criticism, have difficulty with group interactions, and feel socially inept; this picture is very different from that seen in most boys of the same age. On the other hand, girls diagnosed with the hyperactive-impulsive type of ADD are more similar to boys—that is, stubborn, angry, defiant or rebellious, and hyperactive.

Adolescence poses its own problems without ADD. Adding this to the mix can complicate issues. Dr. Nadeau cites three major issues: (1) severe premenstrual syndrome, (2) tremendous concern with peer acceptance, and (3) among hyperactive-impulsive girls, a sense of shame. She notes that because of these issues, it is even more important that home becomes a stabilizing and calming influence and suggests the following guidelines to help with daughters.

Teach your daughters to establish a "quiet zone" in their lives.

Whether shy and withdrawn, or hyper and impulsive, girls with ADD often feel emotionally overwhelmed. They need to learn stress management techniques from an early age, and to understand that they need emotional "time out" to regroup after an upset.

Try to minimize corrections and criticism.

Too often, parents—with the best of intentions—shower girls who have ADD with corrections and criticisms. "Don't let them hurt your feelings like that." "You'd forget your head if it wasn't attached to your shoulders." "How do you expect to go to college with grades like that?" "If you just relaxed, dressed a little better...." These girls, whether loud and rebellious or shy and retiring, typically suffer from low self-esteem. Home is not only an important place to refuel, it is where confidence—so frequently eroded during the day at school—must be rebuilt.

Help them look for ways to excel.

Girls with ADD typically feel that they are "not good at anything." Their distractibility, impulsivity, and disorganization often result in mediocre grades. Likewise, they often don't have the persistence, the "stick-to-it-iveness," to develop skills and talents like many of their friends. Helping girls with ADD find a skill or ability, and then praising and recognizing them for it are terrific positive boosts. Often, the life of an adolescent girl with ADD reaches a positive turning point when she is lucky enough to find an activity that can raise her self-esteem.

Seek medical treatment if PMS is severe.

PMS is something that many females with ADD need to carefully manage throughout their lives. If PMS is severe in adolescence it should be taken seriously and managed carefully. Sometimes severe PMS is managed through the use of antidepressants, with the dosage being varied according to the menstrual cycle.

40

DO CHILDREN OUTGROW ADD?

For years it was thought that children with ADD outgrew this disorder as they went through the stages of puberty. It was believed that there was a lessening of behaviors associated with ADD throughout adolescence and finally they were totally absent in adulthood. Recent research and clinical observations indicate that a substantial number of children with ADD continue to have symptoms of the disorder throughout adulthood. Although the exact number varies, it appears that about 50 percent of children with ADD will continue to have symptoms as adults. Adult ADD is a relatively new area of study, therefore, we know much less than we do about children with ADD. However, there is a growing body of research on the characteristics of this population. One of the leading researchers, Dr. Paul Wender, and his colleagues at the University of Utah Medical Center have described some characteristics of adults with ADD. They caution that the findings are tentative:

1. Attention problems.
2. Hyperactivity.
3. Impulsivity.
4. Mood swings.
5. Disorganization and inability to complete tasks.
6. Short and hot temper.
7. Low stress tolerance.

Many of these characteristics are similar to those observed in children, but they manifest themselves differently in adults.

Attention Problems

Not unlike children with ADD, adults find it difficult to attend to tasks. They cannot concentrate on certain types of materials. Generally, if it is very interesting to them and they are motivated they can concentrate. However, even if the material is necessary for school or a job they cannot always focus on it if the material is not interesting to them. In extreme cases they have a hard time with written material. We know an adult with ADD who says he can read little beyond a local newspaper or a simple magazine because he cannot pay attention. He finds himself turning pages in a book but has no comprehension because, as he says, "his mind drifts off into space." This drifting also occurs in interpersonal relationships. Adults with ADD are frequently told that they are not paying attention to a conversation, direction, story, and so forth. They are not doing so willfully; they simply cannot focus in on what the other person is saying. You may be thinking, "I do that at times." True. We all do. For adults with ADD, however, the persistence of the problem is the defining characteristic.

These adults also report being easily distracted by noises, sights, sounds, almost anything that captures their attention and causes them to have difficulty remaining on task. Like the child who is distracted by every noise in the classroom, these adults find environmental sights and sounds competing for their attention in the work place.

Hyperactivity

In adulthood, hyperactivity takes on a different form. No doubt you've known adults who could not sit still, were always on the go. These are adults who could not sit for a long car ride, a movie, a dinner party. They may engage in a number of habits such as tapping their foot, playing with jewelry, or tapping their fingers. Unlike children, they are not confined to a classroom; however, this behavior can interfere with their job and personal life.

Impulsivity

Adults with ADD tend to act without sufficient thought. You may know the feeling: You're so tired and weary you do something foolish and think about the consequences afterward. This may be a persistent pattern for adults with ADD. Dr. Wender reports that these adults have a hard time dealing with frustration, postponing decisions, and delaying gratification. The consequences can be dire—numerous failures in their personal lives and on the job.

Mood Swings

Moods change rapidly and frequently in adults with ADD. These adults tend to overreact to situations, either positively or negatively, not necessarily based on anything they can pinpoint. For the most part these mood swings are short lived, lasting at most a few days.

Disorganization and Inability to Complete Tasks

Adults with ADD may have trouble organizing minor tasks so that it appears that "nothing ever gets done." They have a hard time setting priorities, both at work and at home. They may never know where they placed an item, fail to return phone calls because they misplaced the message, or appear to be befuddled by difficult tasks that require problem-solving skills.

Short and Hot Temper

The previously described temper tantrums of childhood may persist for some adults with ADD. However, they tend to last for a short time. Some have learned coping mechanisms, but for those that haven't this short fuse can interfere with their social and business life.

Low Stress Tolerance

These adults tend to get overwhelmed rapidly. They report that they have "thin skin" and are easily distressed to the point that they are incapable of responding to a situation. Not surprisingly, as the problem becomes more difficult, so does the level of stress and they become incapacitated.

Dr. Russell A. Barkley, Director of the ADHD Clinic at the University of Massachusetts Medical Center, has also been studying adults with ADD. He has reported that adults have difficulty in academics, employment, and social skills. They may also display anti-social behaviors. He notes, however, that the majority of adults with ADD have learned to compensate and make satisfactory adjustments to adulthood.

The treatment for adults with ADD, as with children, must be comprehensive. At the present time, there are no proven interventions for adults. Medication, behavioral intervention, psychotherapy, and counseling have been employed, but currently it is impossible to state the most effective way to deal with the disorder.

The answer to the original question, "Do children outgrow ADD?," is not so simple. Current research suggests that almost half of the children with ADD will continue to have some of the symptoms through adulthood. And although we are able to identify some characteristics, it is much too early to say that these are definitive traits. Moreover, much more work needs to be done to evaluate the effectiveness of the various interventions that have been proposed.

We often hear parents and teachers say, "They'll out-grow it, so why bother doing anything now." First of all, we are not sure which children are more apt to "outgrow it." And second, the psychological, educational, and financial problems the child will encounter while we are waiting for them to "outgrow it" will be difficult, if not impossible, to overcome. The only proper way to approach the complex problems associated with ADD is early diagnosis by a multi-disciplinary team and a comprehensive treatment plan that is closely monitored by informed parents and competent pro-fessionals.

QUESTIONS AND ANSWERS

Are all children with ADD hyperactive?

No. Many people seem to associate hyperactivity with all attention deficits, but it's only one part. Many children have a hard time concentrating on a task, are impulsive, yet they are not hyperactive. Hyperactivity is an overused term that we feel is used too casually.

What causes ADD?

The basis for ADD is biological. While we don't know exactly why, we do know that the child with ADD comes into the world with this disorder. Due to the behaviors the child engages in and the reactions of others, psychological factors come into place. Therefore, most experts agree that it is caused by an interaction of biological and psychological causes.

Has there been an increase in the number of children with ADD?

The percentage of children with ADD has remained about the same. Experts say about 3-5 percent of school-aged children have the disorder. However, it has gained recognition and higher visibility of late. Some suggest that schools are claiming ADD for a wide variety of school problems.

What do I do if I think my child has ADD?

If you think your child has ADD we suggest you contact a university-based hospital for an evaluation. This will include a medical evaluation, a psychological evaluation, an education evaluation, and a social history. Without a multi-disciplinary evaluation, you may not get the answers you need to deal with your child effectively. If you are not near a university-based hospital, speak to your school and/or pediatrician for a referral to experts who deal with ADD.

Is medication effective in treating ADD?

Experts say that 70-80 percent of people with ADD benefit from medication. Usually, medication is not used alone; behavior management and/or family counseling are also used. There are side effects to medication, therefore you need to monitor your child's behavior in both school and home.

Do food or allergies cause ADD?

Some professionals call for the elimination of certain foods to cure ADD, yet the research has not proven this to be effective. Parents who are concerned about the effect of food on their child's behavior should consult a physician and perhaps have a multidisciplinary evaluation.

What about sugar? I've heard it makes kids hyperactive.

There simply has not been proof that the level of sugar causes ADD. In fact, one expert, Dr. C. Keith Connor, suggests that some children with ADD may need more sugar during certain times of the day.

Do all children with ADD have learning disabilities?

No. Apparently 30 percent of those children with ADD

are also LD. And not all LD students have ADD. This percentage is also about a third.

Are children with ADD classified as special education students?

Under recent legislation (Individuals with Disabilities Education Act), children with ADD can receive special education services if their diagnoses fall within one of three classifications (Learning Disabilities, Emotional Disorders, and Other Health Impaired). ADD is not yet a specific special education category.

Should children with ADD be in a special education classroom?

Most children with ADD are in regular classroom settings and receive special education services depending upon their specific needs. Just because they have ADD does not mean they need to be in a special class.

Are there support groups available for parents?

There are a few groups for parents of children with ADD. One such group, CHADD, provides parents with support and information about children with ADD. It is very important for a parent to join such a group for information and support. It is helpful to learn from others who share your concerns.

Do girls have AD/HD?

Yes, but it appears that AD/HD is diagnosed in boys more often than in girls. Many girls with AD/HD are inattentive and distractible, but their symptoms may not always be as obvious as with boys.

GLOSSARY

Attention deficit disorder (ADD) difficulty in concentrating and staying on task. It may or may not also include hyperactivity.

Attention deficit hyperactivity disorder (ADHD) difficulty in concentrating and staying on task. This term also includes hyperactivity.

Behavior Intervention Plan a systematic plan, based on the functional assessment of behavior, developed and implemented to increase appropriate behaviors and decrease inappropriate behaviors.

Behavior modification techniques used to change behavior. It includes careful observation of behavior and changing the environment to increase appropriate behaviors and decrease inappropriate behaviors.

Central nervous system dysfunction a learning disorder caused by an impairment in brain functions.

Continuous reinforcement reinforcement of a desired behavior every time it happens.

Distractibility the tendency to pay attention to irrelevant information.

Feingold diet a diet that eliminates artificial flavors and artificial colors in an attempt to control hyperactivity.

Hyperactivity excessive motor activity that makes children seem like they are always on the go, restless, and fidgeting.

IDEA (97) Individuals with Disabilities Education Act (Amended 1997). This is the federal law that governs that education of students with special educational needs. It was recently amended in 1997 with changes going into effect July 1, 1999.

Impulsivity acting without thinking of the consequences.

Inclusion the education of students with disabilities in regular education settings.

Individualized Education Program (I.E.P.) a written plan that describes the special education services a student will receive.

Learning disability a term used to describe children with average intelligence who are not achieving up to potential. It is presumed to be due to a central nervous system dysfunction.

Mainstreaming placing children with disabilities within the regular classroom.

Megavitamins treatment of ADD children with pills, capsules, or liquid with extremely large doses of vitamins.

Neurotransmitter the chemicals that transmit messages from one cell of the central nervous system to another.

Positive reinforcement any event that increases the chance a behavior will occur.

Prereferral Intervention a school-based team responsible for developing and implementing instructional and behavioral intervention *prior to* a referral for special education.

Rating scale a ranking of students; behavior as judged by parent or teacher.

Section 504 of the Rehabilitation Act of 1973 states that no individual with a disability (even those not recognized by IDEA) can be denied access to any program or activity because of his or her disability.

Self-esteem feeling of worth and confidence. Having a self-concept that gives you a sense of success.

Social skills skills necessary to meet the basic demands of everyday life.

Appendix A

RESOURCES FOR PARENTS

Organizations

Perhaps one of the most helpful things for parents of children with ADD is to meet with other parents who share their concern. The support of others who have gone through similar experiences is very helpful. Moreover, parents who have "been in the trenches" can be of great assistance to parents who are just discovering that they have a child with ADD. The following is a list of support groups:

ADDA
P.O. Box 972
Mentor, Ohio 44601
(800) 487-2282
Web.site: http://www.add.org

This organization, Attention Deficit Disorder Association, is a referral and information service. Parents can receive the names of professionals in their area who serve the needs of individuals diagnosed with ADD. You can also receive information regarding various aspects of ADD from this organization.

CHADD
8181 Professional Place
Suite 201
Landover, Maryland 20785

(301) 306-7070
(800) 233-4050
Web.site: http://www.chadd.org

This organization has been in the forefront in efforts to provide appropriate services to children with ADD and their families. There are numerous local chapters throughout the country, where parents can find a supportive group of professionals and parents who are knowledgeable in all aspects of ADD. Frequently, they have speakers that focus on a particular aspect of ADD and it's not unusual to find teachers attending these meetings so that they can be better informed. We urge parents to join this organization.

In addition to these organizations some parents may find it useful to contact the Learning Disabilities Association of America if they suspect their child of having a learning disability. They can provide you with useful information and referral services. Their address and phone number is:

Learning Disabilities Association of America
4156 Library Road
Pittsburgh, Pennsylvania 15234
(412) 341-8077
Web.site: http://www.ldanatl.org

Books
Parents can also benefit from reading about ADD. A sampling of books that are helpful are listed below:

Barkley, Russell A. *Attention Deficit Hyperactivity Disorder: A Handbook for Diagnosis and Treatment*, 2nd Ed. New York: The Guilford Press, 1998.

Conner, C.K. *Feeding the Brain*, New York: Plenum Press, 1989.

Fowler, M. *Maybe You Know My Kid: A Parent's Guide to*

Identifying, Understanding, and Helping Your Child with ADHD. Secaucus, New Jersey: Carol Publishing Group, 1991.

Goldstein, S. and Goldstein, M. *Hyperactivity – Why Won't My Child Pay Attention?* New York: Wiley, 1993.

Ingersoll, B. *Your Hyperactive Child: A Parent's Guide to Coping with Attention Deficit Disorders*. New York: Doubleday 1988.

Maghadam, H. *Attention Deficit Disorder: Hyperactivity Revisited: A Concise Source of Information for Parents and Teachers*. Calgary, Alberta, Canada: Detselig Enterprises, 1988.

McNamara, B.E. and McNamara, F.J. *Keys to Parenting a Child with a Learning Disability*. Hauppauge, NY: Barron's, 1995.

Parker, H. *The ADD Hyperactivity Workbook for Parents, Teachers and Kids*. Plantation, Florida: Impact Publication, 1988.

Silver, L.B. *Attention Deficit-Hyperactivity Disorder and Learning Disabilities*. Summit, New Jersey: CIBA-Geigy Pharmaceutical, 1990.

Silver, L.B. *The Misunderstood Child: Understanding and Coping with Your Child's Learning Disability*. New York: Times Books, 1998

Wilens, T.E. *Straight Talk About Psychiatric Medications for Kids*. New York: The Guilford Press, 1999

Wodrich, D.L. *ADHD: What Every Parent Wants to Know*. Baltimore, Maryland: Paul H. Brooks, 1994

Products

Parents should also obtain a catalog from the *A.D.D. Warehouse* (800-233-9273 or 800-ADD-WARE between 8:30 A.M. and 5:00 P.M. EST). This company specializes in products for ADD for parents, educators, and health care professionals. Parents can order books, booklets, audio and video tape programs, as well as books for children and adolescents who have been diagnosed as ADD and want to learn more about it.

Remember, the more you know about ADD the better you are able to help your child.

Appendix B

RESOURCES FOR TEACHERS

I f your child is in a regular classroom setting it is important that her teacher understand ADD. This task is not yours alone; the school should provide training. If your child is in a special education setting, the teacher probably knows about ADD; however, you should always check to see that this is the case. What follows are some resources you can share with teachers. In our experience teachers have been very receptive to parents who provide them with information on ADD.

Harvey C. Parker, Ph.D., co-founder of CHADD and author of *The ADD Hyperactivity Handbook for Schools*, (Plantation, FL: Specialty Press, 1996) provides excellent solutions for common problems of students with ADD. The problems discussed are:

1. Talking excessively
2. Calling out in class
3. Forgetting materials
4. Being off task during independent work
5. Having poor listening skills and not following oral directions
6. Handing in late or uncompleted assignments
7. Turning in sloppy work
8. Failing to complete homework assignments

Teachers will find this resource very useful.

The National Association of School Psychologists provides some ideas for teachers. They include the following guidelines:

What Can I Do as a Teacher?

Approach the ADD child with an understanding of the underlying condition.

- Be aware of the child's limitations. This can help to reduce your frustrations in dealing with the ADD child.
- Try to distinguish between behavior that is noncompliant (the child refuses to do something) and behavior that is the result of ADD (the child can't do something). Treat these behaviors differently. Behaviors that a child can't do require instruction or development of a strategy for compensation. Behavior that is noncompliant requires disciplinary techniques designed to teach compliance and eliminate noncompliance, such as setting specific rules, reinforcing compliance, and removing a privilege or points for noncompliance.
- Interpret group test results cautiously. This child may have rushed through the test, answered impulsively, or have been distracted and not completed the test. Therefore, results may not be useful for determining skill levels for the ADD child.
- Remember that medication is not a panacea. An ADD child who has been placed on medication typically has strikingly improved behavior but often will not have acquired the same skills as other children. Extra instruction may be necessary.
- Take advantage of the energy and spontaneity of the ADD child to help eliminate potential difficulties. For instance, when planning for a class play, the ADD child may be quite

successful at acting out the role of the wind that whooshes across the stage, and may be quite frustrated (and frustrating to you and classmates) if cast as the father who stands quietly and observes before saying his one line.

- Provide for close supervision during unstructured times like recess to help control risk-taking and eliminate potential injuries.

Work with parents and other professionals.

- Ask parents for information about strategies that have been tried with their child in the past.
- Help parents locate resources for dealing with the manifestations of ADD outside of school such as training in child management skills.
- Involve parents in using management strategies such as daily checklists or assignment sheets to help with behavior and assignment completion.
- Use in-school resources. The school psychologist may be willing to observe the ADD child to assist you in identifying specific behaviors or times when interventions would be helpful. Techniques that the school psychologist may be able to assist with include the think aloud program or verbal self-monitoring.
- Refer the ADD child who is displaying significant academic or behavior difficulties for a multi-disciplinary evaluation.
- Monitor changes in the child's behavior. If the ADD student is taking medication, work with the parents and physicians in completing behavior checklists or keeping logs of behaviors to help ensure that medication is providing optimal benefits.

Expect ADD to be an ongoing condition and plan for this chronicity. Behavior management strategies are likely to be necessary on an ongoing basis throughout the elementary grades and often in middle school and high school. Strategies for elementary students require the teacher as manager. As the child gets older, he or she will need help in learning self-management strategies.

Ideas for Elementary Students:

- Special seating near you or slightly apart from classmates may help reduce effects of distractibility.
- Provision of short assignments, or longer assignments broken down into shorter segments, may increase task completion.
- Pairing assignments with a checklist on the child's desk on which he or she can check off completed tasks may help with assignment completion. After showing the child how to make the checklist, provide blank checklists for the child to fill out each day.
- Extra reinforcement will probably be needed if the ADD child is to learn and continue to follow classroom rules. Developing rule-governed behavior requires frequent reinforcement and clear statements of what behavior is being reinforced. Response cost strategies have proved to be effective with many ADD children. Such strategies involve giving points for appropriate behaviors and having the child pay a fine (in points) for inappropriate behaviors. Response cost systems work best when the rules are very specific.
- Organization is particularly difficult for many ADD children. Try using a checklist of what to take home from school each night. Divided notebooks can be useful if the student understands how to use them. Assist with organization of desk or locker space.

Ideas for Secondary Students:

- Since organization often continues to be a problem, assist this student with organizational strategies. For example, help the student learn how to use a divided notebook for different subject areas and check periodically to ensure that this system is being used.

- Have the student purchase a small assignment book and use it daily.
- Help the student learn to make and use checklists. For example, when several assignments need to be completed, have the student list them and check them off as they are completed. Similarly, a checklist of what to take home or bring back to school can be used.
- Plan long-term projects with the student using a calendar with specific dates on which tasks are to be completed. Check back periodically to see how the student is progressing.

Other suggestions are offered by Hawthorn Educational Services in their *ADD Intervention Manual.*

Interventions

1. Reinforce the student for concentrating:
   - (a) Give the student a tangible reward (e.g., classroom privileges, line leading, passing out materials, five minutes free time, etc.) when he or she concentrates, or
   - (b) Give the student an intangible reward (e.g., praise, handshake, smile, etc.) for concentrating.
2. Establish classroom rules (e.g., work on task, work quietly, remain in your seat, finish task, meet task expectations). Reiterate rules often and reinforce students for following rules.
3. Reinforce the student for concentrating on a task for the length of time he or she can be successful. Gradually increase the length of time required for reinforcement.

4. Write a contract with the student specifying what behavior is expected (e.g., concentrating on a task) and what reinforcement will be made available when the terms of the contract have been met.

5. Assess the quality and clarity of directions, explanations, and instructions given to the student.

6. Teach the student to use basic concentration and study skills (e.g., reading for the main idea, note taking, highlighting, outlining, summarizing, studying in an appropriate environment, etc.)

7. Make the subject matter meaningful to the student.

8. Structure the environment in such a way as to reduce distracting stimuli (e.g., place the student in the front row, provide a carrel or quiet place away from distractions, etc.). This is used as a means of reducing distracting stimuli and not as a form of punishment.

9. Follow a less desirable task with a more desirable task, making the completion of the first necessary to perform the second.

10. Break down large tasks into smaller tasks (e.g., assign the student to write an outline for a book report, then the first rough draft, etc.).

11. Assign a peer tutor to work directly with the student to serve as a model for appropriate work habits.

12. Allow natural consequences to occur as a result of the students' inability to concentrate (e.g., work not done or completed inaccurately must be made up during recreational time, not concentrating while people are talking results in not knowing what to do, etc.).

13. Give directions in a variety of ways to increase the probability of understanding (e.g., if the student

fails to understand verbal directions, present them in written form).

14. Provide clearly stated directions, written or verbal (i.e., make directions as simple and concrete as possible).

15. Reduce directions to steps (e.g., give the student each additional step after completion of the previous step).

16. Make certain the student knows that directions will only be given once.

17. Try various groupings in order to determine the situation in which the student can concentrate most easily.

18. Separate the student from the peers who may be encouraging or stimulating the inappropriate behavior.

19. Reinforce the student for beginning, staying on, and completing assignments.

20. Assign the student shorter tasks and gradually increase the number over time as he or she demonstrates success.

21. Use a variety of high interest means to communicate with the students (e.g., auditory, visual, manipulatives, etc.)

22. Present assignments in small amounts (e.g., assign 10 problems, use pages removed from workbooks, etc.)

23. Make certain that the student's academic tasks are on his or her ability level.

24. Teach the student note taking skills (e.g., copy main ideas from the chalkboard, identify main ideas from lectures, condense statements into a few key words, etc.).

25. Maintain physical contact with the student while

talking to him or her (e.g., touch the student's hand or shoulder).

26. Require the student to make eye contact while delivering information to him or her.

27. Deliver one-, two-, and three-step directions to the student, increasing the number of steps as the student demonstrates success in concentrating.

28. Have the student participate in games requiring varying lengths of concentration (e.g., tic-tac-toe, checkers, chess, etc.).

29. Reduce distracting stimuli in and around the student's desk (e.g., materials in the desk, on the desk, etc.).

30. Seat the student close to the source of information.

31. Highlight or underline important information the student reads (e.g., directions, reading assignments, math word problems, etc.)

32. Tell the student what to listen for when being given directions, receiving information, etc.

33. Make certain the student knows what to look for when he or she is reading (e.g., main characters, main ideas, sequence of events, etc.).

34. Provide the student with appropriate time limits for the completion of assignments.

35. Maintain visibility to and from the student at all times in order to monitor the student's concentration.

36. Provide the student with a prompt when he or she is off task (e.g., move close to the student, speak to the student, etc.).

Appendix C

~~~~~~

RESOURCES FOR SIBLINGS

Newsletters

Brakes: The Interactive Newsletter for Kids with ADHD

> Magination Press
> 19 Union Square West
> New York, NY 10003
> (800) 825-3089

The National Association of Sibling Programs Newsletter. A newsletter with useful information and activities related to news workshops throughout the country for siblings. Contact:

> Sibling Support Project
> Children's Hospital and Medical Center
> Seattle, WA 98002

The Sibling Information Network Newsletter. Published on a quarterly basis, it provides information for and about siblings of people with disabilities. Contact:

> Sibling Information Network
> The A.J. Pappanikou Center on
>   Special Educational Rehabilitation:
> A University Affiliated Program
> Main Office
> 991 Main St.
> East Hartford, CT 06108

Books

Baver, K. *Active Andy: An Elementary School Child's Guide to Understanding AD/HD*. Wauwatusa: IMDW Publisher, 1993

Provides helpful tips for children.

Meyer, D.J., Vadascy, P.F. & Kewell, R.R. *Living with a Brother or Sister with Special Needs*. Seattle, Washington: University of Washington Press, 1985.

This book is most appropriate for siblings ages eight through thirteen. It discusses a variety of disabilities, and it presents strategies that will assist siblings in expressing their feelings.

Parker, R. *Slam Dunk*. Plantation, Florida: Specialty Press, 1995.

Provides an understanding of ADD; geared for school-aged children.

Sullivan, M.B., Brightman, J. & Blatt, J. *Feeling Free*. Reading, Massachusetts: Addison-Wesley, 1979.

An activity book with short stories and accounts written by children with learning problems or physical disabilities.

Products

Skills for Special Sibs: Living with Your Handicapped Brother or Sister. (1980). Video, 3/4 inch VHF, color, 13 minutes.

This tape is appropriate for the elementary level child and provides a wide variety of skills for siblings, such as praising, ignoring, expressing anger, that are useful in sibling interaction. It is distributed by:

Child Development Division
Dept. of Pediatrics/Division of Biomedical
    Communication
University of Texas Medical Branch at Galveston,
Galveston, TX 77550

INDEX